The Art of Creative Thinking

THE ART OF CREATIVE THINKING

ROBERT W. OLSON

PERENNIAL LIBRARY

Harper & Row, Publishers
New York, Cambridge, Philadelphia, San Francisco, Washington
London, Mexico City, São Paulo, Singapore, Sydney

A paperback edition of this work was originally published in 1980 by Harper & Row, Publishers, Inc.

Portions of this work originally appeared in *Money Tree*.

First PERENNIAL LIBRARY edition published 1986.

Library of Congress Cataloging-in-Publication Data

Olson, Robert Wallace, 1940–
     The art of creative thinking.

     "Perennial library."
     Bibliography: p.
     1. Creative thinking. 2. Success. I. Title.
BF408.O46   153.3′5   79-2745
ISBN 0-06-097051-0 (pbk.)

86 87 88 89 90 MPC 10 9 8 7 6 5 4 3 2 1

To people willing to work toward developing
their own creativity and to try to make a positive
contribution to the well-being of man. And to
Lawnee, Robert and Vawnee for their special contribution to the development of my creativity

PREFACE

For the past two decades I have been intrigued by two fascinating questions of creativity. Why don't people use more of their creativity? And, how can people become more creative?

I used to think of creativity as something rather unusual, something that should be applied to problems such as putting man on the moon or coming up with a new social program here on earth. However, the more I utilize my own creativity and study the use of the creativity of other people, the more I believe that it is one of the most powerful and ordinary tools of man.

The techniques presented in this book can be used to help you solve ordinary, everyday problems, like what should I buy someone for their birthday, as well as professional ones, such as in what ways can a cheap source of power be developed for the world.

Frequently books written in the field of creativity are written about the creativity of others and are designed for professional psychologists. They are difficult to understand and offer little help to those who wish to become more creative and to do something with their creativity. This book is designed to be of value to professionals in areas such as business, psychology, education and engineering, and to lay persons who are interested in not only understanding the creative thinking process, but also want to better utilize their present abilities and to become more creative.

This book is based on research which I have conducted during the past ten years which was focused on discovering the approaches successful people use to create, finding existing techniques and developing new ones to aid people who want to become more creative. In addition to this research, I have utilized my personal experience as a nuclear engineer, project engineer, educator, businessman and psychologist. The techniques and ideas presented in this book have been tested and refined on thousands of people in workshops, seminars and college classes.

I want to express my gratitude to the many people who have contributed to the development of this book. I want to thank my wife, Vawnee, and children, Robert and Lawnee, for their understanding support of my work and their enrichment of my creativity; the many college and university students, friends, business leaders, scientists and artists who have made valuable contributions to my work; artist Kevin Fagan for collaborating with me to develop the cartoons and illustrations; Helen Baxter for typing assistance. I especially wish to thank Doug Nash, Max Schreiber, Philip Rogers and Robert Lombardi for their encouragement and help.

This book was enjoyable to write and it helped me become more creative. I hope it provides you with as much pleasure and creative growth as it did me.

Robert W. Olson, Ph.D.
Mission Viejo, California

Postscript:

At 23, Kevin Fagan, the cartoonist-illustrator for this book, has become a creative success as America's youngest syndicated cartoonist. His comic strip, "Drabble," is read by millions of people from coast to coast in newspapers such as the <u>Washington Post</u>, <u>Chicago Sun Times</u>, <u>Seattle Times</u>, and <u>Toronto Globe</u>.

The cartoons and illustrations in this book represent his first professional work. I have observed him informally utilize many of the creative thinking techniques described in this book to help develop his own creativity. It has been a great thrill for me to watch Kevin progress from a college newspaper cartoonist to a successful syndicated cartoonist. Congratulations, Kevin!

Contents

Illustrations

INTRODUCTION

This book is designed to help you nurture, develop, and exercise
your creativity. It offers you tools for recognizing opportunities,
developing fresh insight into problems and original, innovative solutions to the challenging problems in life. It helps you "do" something
with your creativity, instead of merely talking, reading, or thinking
about it.

Our society is ever-changing and multi-dimensional. It needs the
creative talents of each and every one of us. The pace of change in
business, education, and life in general continues to increase. Instead of treating rapid change as a threat, we can treat it as an oppor-
tunity--an opportunity to utilize our creativity, to improve ourselves
and to improve the world within which we live.

Throughout history, many problems have been solved by chance or
ignored. But now, because our society is dynamic and complex, we face
more problems than ever before. Therefore, we must be deliberate and
creative in our approach to solving problems if we are to prosper. We
need to accelerate and give direction to our natural problem-solving
methods.

This book offers no answers to the problems which we face. It
offers processes, techniques, and insights which are valuable in finding answers to any problem--whether it is a small or large problem,
whether it is a problem we face at home or on the job, or whether it is
one which is faced by mankind on earth.

The presentation of practical processes and techniques for creative
problem solving rather than answers is consistent with contemporary

education in colleges and universities throughout the country. For example, only half of the engineering knowledge learned in colleges today will be valid in five to ten years because of the rapid changes and discoveries occurring in our technological society. Therefore, it is as important to learn how to solve problems and how to face a new and changing world as it is to memorize an established body of knowledge.

Your life can be spent acquiring more and more facts and knowledge, yet the end product may be an aged and immature child still unable to think and act in a creative, effective, and productive manner. Or, your life can be successful, exciting, and productive when you develop your creative resources and make creative thinking an integral part of your life.

This book is designed to help you gain control of your life and your creativity, instead of allowing your life and creativity to control you. Instead of letting the pace and pressure of everyday life push you off the track causing you to lose sight of the important challenges of life, this book can help you recognize these challenges, face them and conquer them.

Probably the greatest, most powerful resource on earth today and the most tremendous source of energy is within individual people. Natural resources for energy, such as gas and oil, are being exhausted. The most important and powerful energy of all is barely being tapped. That is the creative energy of the mind. Our creative thinking energy can help people find ways to multiply the world's physical resources and use them more effectively.

Professional people who have developed creative capacities often use them in a limited, narrow fashion. For example, frequently the engineer is creative only when he is inventing or designing but not while writing reports, interacting with other people, or at home. Artists are often only creative when they wear their berets. They don't visualize other problems not related to art which surround them as challenges and opportunities. They don't approach them with the same creative vigor.

Naturally we must focus our energies; we must concentrate our efforts on one area at a time, whether it be our work, church, or family. However, we don't have to completely ignore the other important challenges and opportunities in our life and approach them in a rigid, habitual and unimaginative way.

"To live is to have problems and to solve problems is to grow intellectually," stated J. P. Guilford, a psychologist. Problem solving is the central mental activity of people. It has been said that new computers can do everything but think--this makes them almost human. We don't often think creatively. However, we can think creatively in a fashion that will make us more powerful than computers. We can creatively originate large numbers of new diverse solution ideas to problems. Computers are usually limited to producing a few solution ideas which are similar to each other.

It is commonly felt that creative opportunity and meaningful problems exist in other people's lives, on other jobs, and in other fields, but that the opportunity for improvement in our own job or life is pretty well exhausted. We may feel that only through pure luck will we be able to make a creative contribution in our own job or life. This is not true--creative opportunities exist all around us; we need to learn to see and recognize them.

-3-

Creativity can be taught. Research at the State University of New York at Buffalo revealed that by the end of one class in creativity the students had almost doubled their creative thinking ability. Many companies, such as IBM and General Electric, have implemented programs within their companies to stimulate and develop creativity.

Learning the art of creative problem solving is similar to learning other kinds of skills such as the skill of playing tennis, a physical rather than mental skill. To learn to play tennis a person must master how to hold the racket, how to follow through with their stroke, and the ability to keep their eye on the ball. These skills are very useful to beginning as well as advanced tennis players. Even the most advanced tennis players continue to work on the fundamentals of the game. In the advanced stages of playing tennis, individuals with tremendous skill must learn to capitalize on their uniqueness as a person, their unique muscle structure, hand size, coordination, and emotional stability, to maximize their particular way of playing the game. However, in the beginning, most professional tennis players took lessons and learned how others had played before them. They learned some of the standard successful techniques of the game.

Similarly, to learn creative problem solving, you need to learn the strokes of the game, the patterns, approaches, techniques used by successfully creative people. Fundamental patterns and techniques are important for beginners to attempt and for the advanced creative thinker to continue to work on. As with tennis, when you become confident with the fundamentals, you learn to modify and to select those particular skills that are most appropriate for your particular mental abilities, for your particular memory, for your particular interests and motivations, speed of thinking, and depth of thinking.

In this book, the DO IT process and techniques for creatively solving problems are emphasized as a way to help you become more creative. As William James once noted, "In the dim background of mind we know what we ought to be doing but somehow we cannot start. Every moment we expect the spell to break, but it continues pulse after pulse and we float with it." One of the purposes of the DO IT process and techniques is to help provide you with a starting point, to help you see patterns in problem solving which have been used successfully by other creative people.

The DO IT process and techniques combine the systematic approaches used by engineers and businessmen with the intuitive approaches used by artists and composers. They are based on the methods used by great creative artists, scientists, musicians and businessmen. In addition, they include essential components of established creative ideation techniques such as brainstorming and synectics. They are not the only way to become more creative; they are one way. But they can be used as a beginning to provide you with a basis for your own way.

The DO IT process is not some "far out" approach that can only be used by monks isolated on a mountain top devoting their full life to creative thinking. It is a process which is in close contact with reality, that can be used quickly or over a long period of time. It is sufficiently different from everyday approaches to thinking to help you originate fresh, new, and exciting insights into and solutions to problems. Yet it is similar enough to everyday approaches that you don't need to completely abandon your usual approach to problem solving.

People who use the DO IT process and techniques tend to become

more open. They tend to trust their own ideas and those of other people more. They tend to be more willing to face problems and are more
self-confident. They tend to identify problems more easily and solve
them better. They tend to be excited about what they are doing and
produce creative results.

We are in a society where people expect instant results. An organization will say "Come to my weekend seminar and you'll be transformed into a human being with a thousand percent greater potential,
and you will come in contact with your true self and you'll be able to
do anything you want to do." Miracles are not in the fabric of the
DO IT process and techniques. However, they can significantly develop
and help you "do" something with your creativity.

Mark Twain once wrote that a visitor to heaven asked Saint Peter
if he might meet the greatest general who had ever lived. Saint Peter
pointed to a nearby angel. The visitor protested that he had known
that man, who was not a general but only a cobbler. "Oh yes," replied
Saint Peter, "but if he had been a general he would have been the
greatest of them all." The cobbler did not develop his creative potential to its fullest.

Problem solving is a central activity in life, whether it's the
problem of painting a new picture or originating a new invention. Don't
imitate the past. Create a future, a better tomorrow. Work smarter,
not harder. In the process of solving problems creatively, you not only
produce something but you become something as well.

Reading this book, like reading any book about a skill such as
painting or tennis, will provide you with insights necessary to become

more creative. However, to actually become creative, try the exercises

and apply the results to your own life.

P A R T   I

B A C K G R O U N D

    To become more creative, it is beneficial to begin by briefly ex-
ploring the questions: "What is creativity?" "Why do people create?"
"What are the obstacles to becoming more creative?" "What are creative
people like?" "What is natural creativity?" "How can people be deliberately creative?" and "How can people better recognize creative
problems, challenges and opportunities?"

Chapter 1

WHAT IS CREATIVITY?

Creativity is the ability to create. No single, generally acceptable statement of what constitutes a creation exists. A creation to
one person might mean discovering a new planet, to another playing the
piano or tennis well, to another painting unusually good pictures, or
to another it might simply mean trying something new. The psychologist
Abraham Maslow stated that a first-rate soup is more creative than a
second-rate painting.

For the purpose of research on creative thinking, creativity is
often considered to consist of two elements: fluency and flexibility.
Fluency is evidenced by the ability to smoothly and rapidly produce a
large number of solution ideas for a problem. On a creativity test for
fluency, a person might be asked to list all the possible uses of a
coat hanger, brick, or paper clip during a fixed period of time.

Flexibility generally refers to the capability of finding divergent, unusual solution ideas for a problem. For example, a divergent
solution idea for improving the method of opening doors would be to
locate the door knob on the wall adjacent to the door instead of on the
door itself. Flexible thinking is also evidenced by the ability to
find divergent uses for existing products. For example, a flexible
thinker might recognize that a paper clip can do more than clip things;
it can also be used to scrape, pick and stir.

Creativity is considered by some to be any ability which leads to
a new idea or fresh insight. In one dictionary creativity is presented
as being a process which produces something which would not naturally

evolve or that is not made by ordinary means. But who is to decide what is new or fresh, ordinary or natural?

Creativity could be thought of as the ability to break from rigid habits, the defeat of habit by originality. However, many people have the rigid habit of being creative.

Many people feel that creativity is simply the ability to make new combinations of objects, numbers, colors, notes, chemicals, and words which satisfy some need or desire. For example, a clock radio is the combination of a clock and a radio.

Goethe wrote that there is nothing more fearful than creativity without taste. Woody Allen, in his book Without Feathers, humorously describes a dentist who used imagination without taste. He made a new dental bridge as he "felt it" and not to fit the customer's "ridiculous" mouth. He didn't want to work like a "common tradesman!" The bridge was enormous and billowing, with wild explosive teeth flaring out in every direction like fire! He found it beautiful and was "wracked with despair" because the customer was upset that it wouldn't fit her mouth!

The dentist may have felt creative. However, the customer deemed him simply incompetent and perhaps dangerous. Many definitions of creativity require that the end product be tasteful or have value. But who is to decide what is tasteful or valuable?

Perhaps the driver's response to the police officer's ticket in illustration 1 is creative. If he has properly gauged his "creative remark" to the uniqueness of the traffic violation and the police officer involved, his remark may succeed in saving him from a ticket and his efforts will be considered creative. If his remark doesn't work and he still gets a ticket, his remark will be judged by others as being stupid, silly, or worse. Ideas labeled creative are usually successful in addition to being new.

Questionable Creativity
Illustration 1

Creativity may be considered as the ability to be a good listener, listening to ideas coming from the outside world and the ones coming from the inside or unconscious world. Creativity has been defined as the experience of expressing and actualizing one's individual identity in an integrated form in communion with one's self, with nature, and with other people.

In this creative thinking text the term creativity is used to refer to the ability in an individual which relies on his uniqueness to pro- duce new ideas and fresh insights which are of value to that individual. Someone else may have already thought of the idea or may not value it. However, people are still being creative if they discover it for them- selves and it satisfies one of their needs or desires.

Creative Ideas

The yardstick used most often to establish the creativity of a person is the value of one's creative ideas. A variety of ideas of varying value which are considered creative follows:

An employee of the State of California won a $5,500 award of merit for a creative idea that saved the state $110,000. His creative idea was how to change the reflective signs used in highway construction zones - saying "Men Working" and "Detour Ahead" - from yellow to orange, to comply with new federal rules.

The state had concluded that it must junk the yellow signs and buy new ones because the aluminum faced reflective sheeting could not be painted. The employee's creative contribution was to develop a way to paint the yellow signs with a translucent red paste which makes them look orange.

One of my college students discovered a major break in the water line leading to his home. He had to shut off the water but could not get the parts to fix it until the next day. He didn't want to be without water for 24 hours. His creative solution was to attach a hose between his neighbor's hose bib (with their concurrence) and one to his. This provided a supply of hot and cold running water directly into his home for this emergency period.

Another student responded to his girl friend's complaints of rotting macrame by developing a drain cup. The cup collects water which drains from the plant's pot after watering. The cup is held in position by the bill of the cup which is wedged in between the pot and the bottom of the macrame (see illustration 2). His initial cup was made from a plastic picnic cup to which he Scotch-taped a plastic bill to collect

-14-

the water. It worked so well that he has manufactured and sold thousands of them through retail outlets.

Drain Cup
Illustration 2

Many of us have experienced the aggravation of pulling a garden hose around a garden corner only to find that it drags over into the garden and damages some of the plants. A stake with a little bulge on it was developed by one of my students to prevent this (see illustration 3) from occurring. It works. It's not patentable. Almost anyone could have developed an equally good idea. What was creative about this idea was that, unlike most of us who simply live with aggravations, action was taken to overcome an aggravation.

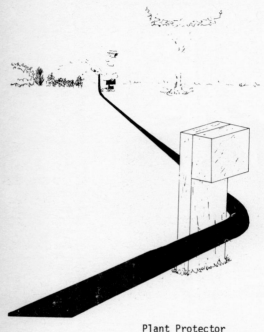

Plant Protector
Illustration 3

None of these creative ideas are sufficient in themselves to say that their originators are truly creative and ready to join the ranks of Wolfe, Einstein and Picasso. However, each is a new idea which is of value and fresh to the individual involved. Each of these creative ideas is a stepping stone to many more and better creative ideas.

Creativity Grows with Exercise!

1. Find three written definitions of creativity other than those mentioned in this text. Specify the source of each definition and

-16-

discuss how the definitions differ.

2. Write your own personal brief definition of creativity.

3. Ask three people for their definition of creativity. Discuss how their definitions differ from a dictionary definition.

4. Describe several ideas or things you have done which you consider to be creative.

5. List several ideas which you consider to be uncreative.

6. Why can't creativity be easily defined?

7. List five words similar to creativity.

8. List five words which are the opposite of creativity.

9. Find two newspaper and/or magazine articles which demonstrate someone's creativity. Write your reasons for selecting each article.

10. Are creative people that you know or have read about creative in most areas of their lives or just in the area where they received recognizition for being creative? Why?

11. What things around you do you see that indicate that people are creative?

12. In what ways is driving down a street engulfed in fog like making a decision with only one idea?

Chapter 2

WHY DO PEOPLE CREATE?

Perhaps this chapter should be entitled why people want to create
or should create instead of why do they create. In general, people
dance to the tune of their habits, follow the callings of our biologi-
cal system and simply "get through the day." The writer, George
Bernard Shaw, observed "Few people think more than two or three times
a year. I've made an international reputation for myself by thinking
once or twice a week." Even if people aren't frequently creative,
they all, to varying extents, are driven by an inner need to be creative.

Humans, of all the creatures on earth, can significantly change
their own pattern of behavior, plan their own destiny and generate
creative ideas by act of will. Perhaps people create because they can
create. They seem to have an urge to expand, develop and mature--to
become all that they are capable of becoming.

The psychologist, Abraham Maslow, divided the needs of people into
the categories of physiological (food, water and sex), safety (security,
order and stability), love and belongingness and esteem (self-respect
and a feeling of success), and self-actualization (creating and making
the most of one's abilites). If these are people's needs, it would
appear that they create for a variety of reasons depending upon their
particular needs at the moment. People may, in the event of war, create
to develop a weapon for self-protection (safety). They may, if they are
lonely, create to fulfill a need for the love and affection of other
people, or they may create as a result of their inner drive to actualize

-19-

their abilities (become their potentials).

Robert Louis Stevenson wrote, "To be what we are, and to become what we are capable of becoming is the only end of life." The mainspring of creativity appears to be the central tendency of man to try to become his potentialities and express his being.

On the other hand, psychologists such as B. F. Skinner feel that people are not responsible for their conduct; they are not to blame when they aren't being creative or deserving of credit when they are creative. They are simply creatures of their environments. What they do depends on what types of stimuli are in their environment. If their environment stimulates and rewards their creativity, they will be creative.

Benefits From Creating

Psychologists cannot agree on the basic needs and motives people have for creating. However, more observable tangible rewards can be identified which motivate people to create. Paul Davies, President of Educational Data System, made the following comments following a creative problem solving session which I had conducted for his company. He wrote, "The sessions served two useful functions for our company: First, they generated many new and useful ideas on the specific problem. Secondly, they created an enthusiasm within the company for the use of creativity techniques and demonstrated how to apply them. We plan to make these techniques a permanent and central part of our approach to all kinds of corporate problems. And, we expect results -- in profits, savings, new corporate directions, and increased enthusiasm of our people. One of the best things about creativity is that it gets everyone really thinking about the problem and pulling together. This in itself fully justifies the effort."

Research at the University of New York at Buffalo has shown that
a course in creativity tends to increase leadership ability, persistence
and initiative as well as creativity. Creating helps people develop
new interests in work, leisure and life in general. The president of
a large company reported that you can pay an employee lots of money
but if you don't stimulate his creativity he is not going to be very
effective.

People who become more creative become more open-minded to their
own ideas (have greater faith in them) and the ideas of others. They
learn to delay judgment. Their initiative and resourcefulness are increased. Problems are generally recognized earlier and solved in a
timely, creative fashion. Likewise, opportunities are generally recognized and taken advantage of sooner. Procrastination, which often
results from the awesome appearance of problems, is reduced.

Creating helps develop our mental resources--our most exciting
resource. As Samuel Johnson said, "Curiosity is one of the most permanent
and certain characteristics of a vigorous mind." People obtain greater
self-acceptance and confidence which also results in a more enthusiastic
acceptance of responsibility.

An intracompany bulletin of the Ethyl Corporation pointed out that
while the purpose of creative problem-solving sessions is to generate
ideas, which they definitely accomplish, the by-products of such sessions can be many. They can be tools for improving morale; they can
provide a method of discovering what people think about supervisory
problems; and they can help supervisors gain a better understanding of
each other. As one man said after one of these sessions, "I gained a

-21-

new respect for each man in the session. It was a novel and elevating experience to me."

One researcher even found that creativity and fear of death are intricately linked. "The more complete one's life is, the more one's destiny and one's creative capacities are fulfilled, the less one fears death," observed Marburg Goodman of Jersey City (N.J.) State College, after 623 in-depth interviews with creative people and others.

Alexander Lowen, in the book Pleasure, stresses that pleasure provides the motivation and energy for a creative approach to life, which in turn increases the pleasure and joy of living. It introduces new excitement and offers new channels for self-expression.

Carl Rogers, in Toward a Theory of Creativity, wrote that genuinely creative adaption seems to represent the only possible way that man can keep abreast of the kaleidoscopic changes in the world. Alvin Toffler, in the book Future Shock, observed that change is not merely necessary to life--it is life.

Even though some humorous observers feel that people's need to create stems from their innate desire to "live beyond their income," research reveals that people create because of basic needs such as safety, love and esteeem. They are also motivated to create by their environment and the specific beneficial results of being creative such as a more exciting life, greater self-confidence, pleasure in living and a chance to make the most of their abilities. Perhaps the greatest benefit of all is not the joy of being creative but the joy of becoming more creative.

Creativity Grows With Exercise!

1. Ask three people why they feel people create. Discuss the results.

2. Discuss the statement "When you create something, you become something as well."

3. List five possible reasons you think Charles Kettering may have had for inventing the automatic starter for the automobile.

4. List five reasons Picasso may have had for creating his art.

5. List ten reasons F. L. Wright may have had for creating his architecture.

6. List ten reasons why you are reading this book on creativity.

7. List the benefits that the creative people mentioned in problems three through five may have received as a result of their creative efforts.

8. What specific benefits, in addition to those mentioned in this chapter, might result when people create?

Chapter 3

OBSTACLES TO BECOMING MORE CREATIVE

One approach to problem solving is to define the problem, identify
the obstacles to solving the problem and then decide how to overcome
each obstacle. The central problem to be solved in this text is how to
help you become more creative. The solution to this problem depends on
your ability to overcome your obstacles to creative thinking. Obstacles
which you might face include habit, limited availability of time and
energy, your environment, need for immediate solutions, criticism by
others, fear of failure, difficulty in recognizing problems, poor attitudes, complacency and difficulty in doing directed mental work. As
you read this chapter, try to identify the obstacles which most retard
your creativity.

Habit

"Those opposed to my idea please signify by saying 'I Resign!'"
sneered a supervisor. Most obstacles to becoming more creative are not
this obvious. Most obstacles are the result of our own unchanging,
habitual approach to life.

The philosopher, William James, wrote "Ninety-nine hundredths or
possibly nine hundred and ninety-nine thousandths of our activity is purely
automatic and habitual, from our rising in the morning to our lying
down each night. Our dressing and undressing, our eating and drinking,
our greetings and partings, even most forms of our common speech, are
things of a type so fixed by repetition as almost to be classed as
reflex actions." Habit is generally considered to be an uncreative,
stereotyped form of response. It is doing the same thing always in the

same way, under the same conditions. In illustration 4, Charlie Creator's commitment to <u>always</u> use his "Be Creative" sign to stimulate creativity may reduce his own creativity.

Unrecognized Habit
Illustration 4

Habits are reactions and responses which we have learned to perform automatically without having to think or decide. Habits can make us eat when we are not hungry, sleep when we are not tired, yell when we aren't mad and discard good ideas without giving them a chance.

To gain a better understanding of the impact of habit on our lives, fold your arms in front of you. Is your right or left wrist on top? Research has shown that roughly half of all people fold their arms with their right wrist on top. Now, try to fold your arms with the opposite wrist on top. Most people find this to be uncomfortable or difficult. Perhaps it was chance which determined which wrist each person put on top initially. It is habit which tends to keep it there.

It is usually difficult and uncomfortable to change any habit. For better or worse they continue on. An established habit is as comfortable as an old shoe. It feels good and has comfortably shaped itself to our foot. So when we try something new, often it's like trying a new

pair of shoes. Even if we like the new experience, we are usually uncomfortable with it at first.

For another encounter with habit, visualize (or better yet get)
six toothpicks of equal length. Try to arrange them into four triangles
with sides of length equal to that of a toothpick. Stop reading and try
it. You learn more by doing than by observing. Try many different possibilities. Don't feel bad if you didn't find a solution immediately.
Most people don't.

The primary barrier to the solution of this problem, beyond the
fact that many people give up too easily, is the habit of two dimension-
al (no depth) visualization. Try to solve the problem again. This time
use actual toothpicks and think in three dimensions. The solution is a
tetrahedron. A tetrahedron is like a pyramid with a triangular base
which has sides of equal length.

Habitual ways of viewing objects may lead to an obstacle called
functional fixation. A friend of mine experienced it while camping. He
forgot to bring, and could not find, a funnel to help pour gas from his
gasoline can into the tank of his camping stove. He decided to solve
this problem by simply pouring the gas carefully into the tank and hop-
ing that little gas would spill. He was interrupted during his efforts
by a friend who offered a better solution to his problem. She recommended that he simply cut a small hole in the corner of a styrofoam
coffee cup and use it as a funnel. It worked. He was a victim of functional fixation--only a standard funnel can be used to funnel gas, not
a coffee cup.

William James wrote "Genius, in truth, means little more than the
faculty of perceiving in an unhabitual way." Habits come in many forms

and affect not only thinking and seeing but also the sense of smell, feel, taste, and sound. The specific obstacles to becoming more creative discussed in this book are primarily "thinking" types of obstacles. They are all related to the fact that we have mental habits and to some of the reasons for having and keeping them. Even our unwillingness to take the time required to be and become more creative is due in part to habit.

Time

But I don't have time to be creative, especially now! When deadlines are knocking at your door and results are demanded, it's hard to even remember to be creative let alone take the time necessary to be creative. On the other hand, people who have time to be more creative take it out of the same 24 hours per day allocated to everyone else. They have overcome their habit of acting immediately without first thinking.

The logger sawing the large pile of logs in illustration 5 may feel that he doesn't have time to think of a more creative way to cut the logs. He has too much work to do. He doesn't even have time to sharpen his saw and thereby greatly reduce the time he must spend to cut the logs. Most people are like this logger; they are not willing to invest that little extra time to sharpen their creativity or to use it. Time which could pay such great dividends and ultimately save time. Henry Ford once remarked that "the more you think, the more time you have."

Uncreative Use of Time
Illustration 5

Overwhelmed by Problems

When we are faced with the problem of opening a door, we approach
it automatically without deciding how to grip the knob, how fast to turn
it, and when to release it. If we didn't approach problems like this
habitually, we would be overwhelmed with problems and would not be able
to cope with our environment. Most of us don't consider opening a door
to be a problem which overloads our mental apparatus because we do it
habitually. However, some of us feel that we face so many problems
which are important that we don't have enough time or energy to solve
any of them creatively. So, we ignore all problems and refuse to let
them enter our conscious mind.

Most professional people face a similar problem overload in their
work. Competent, successful professional people don't just give up or
solve every problem uncreatively. They usually consciously or unconsciously order their problems, challenges, goals and opportunities

according to priorities and in effect do "first things first." Often
they don't even get to the problems which are unimportant. However,
they are able to effectively and creatively solve those problems which
are the most important.

It is easy to be overwhelmed by problems especially if we realize
that problems are defined, in the broadest sense, as the difference
between what is and what we want to be. Using this definition, if we
are creative and want to be more creative, we have a problem. If we
are at home and want to get to work, we have a problem. If we are poor
and want to be rich, or sad and want to be happy, we have a problem.

Many of these problems we ignore or solve habitually. If we
choose to, we can view all problems as creative challenges. However,
if we do, we are in danger of facing a problem overload. Our mind
could be faced with so many problems that it would be unable to function
well. Therefore, to become more creative, we must identify and priori-
tize our problems. Then we can creatively solve at least a few of
them--the important ones creatively.

No Problems

Everything of importance has been said and done! Every good invention invented! Every good idea has been thought! Every worthwhile picture taken or printed! Every symphony composed (see illustration 6).
No problems, challenges, needs or opportunities exist in my life!

Lord Rutherford, a prominent nuclear scientist, wrote "The energy
produced by the breaking down of the atom is a very poor kind of thing.
Anyone who expects a source of power from this transformation of these
atoms is talking moonshine." A few years later, usable energy was being
generated by the atom. Now nuclear power is one of our prime new sources

of electrical power. Often we don't feel problems and opportunities
exist because the "experts" have all the answers or have said it can't
be done.

GEE, I'D LIKE TO WRITE ANOTHER SYMPHONY,
BUT IT SEEMS LIKE EVERYTHING'S ALREADY
BEEN WRITTEN.

No Problems
Illustration 6

We are problem-solving creatures, constantly facing and solving
problems. If our problems are solved automatically or habitually, they
may never be recognized as problems and we may feel that we have no
problems. For example, most people tend to habitually go to bed at a
particular time of night even though they may not get enough sleep so
they don't even consider that to be a possible problem. This is probably because their unconscious priority system is satisfied that this
problem has been solved well enough and that other more important problems need their attention. Once we solve a problem, we tend to think
it has been solved forever, and we use the solution as if it were the

best solution.

For example, if we greeted people we know and like by "hello" ten years ago, we are probably using that same greeting today. If we chose one occupation as the solution to our livelihood problem, we are probably still using that same solution; we are still working on the same job today. A very important source of being creative is to occasionally reexamine our solutions and recognize the problems we face which are caused by solutions which aren't working well.

Many people only consider "on the job problems" to be worthy of creative effort -- problems like how to design a part, sell a customer or paint a picture. Whereas, all problems offer a creative challenge and the opportunity to grow creatively.

Fear of Failure

To turn off the television and walk outside involves possible failure. For example, we may fall and injure ourselves. We can lose our lives to the "tube" or some other "safe" activities but suffer no great pain or anxiety in the process. Or, we can face the exciting challenge of life with the risk of occasional failure. In fact, we are guaranteed some failure when we face life.

Writer, Ray Bradbury, once said that life is "trying things to see if they work." He refers to an exciting life where the rewards of living in the real world far outweigh the possible failures of trying. We can avoid failure and creativity in many ways; by over-conforming, never trying anything different, making sure that we use only proven ideas and walking only worn paths. We thus avoid small failures. However, we become failures as human beings. We become incapable of growing creatively beyond past habits and instincts.

Failure can take the form of ostracism, criticism, loss of time, loss of income or injury. However, nothing is more of a failure than failing to try.

Many people are other directed. They spend their time and energy trying to avoid failure by always trying to see how they appear to others. As a result, they rarely have the time or energy to see anything else.

My business is doing well. I am making a profit. I am fairly happy with my life. Complacency and comfort with the status quo keep us from growing creatively and are often caused by our fear of failure.

The mind is often referred to as an "emergency organ" only used when the threat of punishment or the reward is large. When all else fails, try thinking. Unfortunately, by the time its "emergency" is big enough, it is often too late (see illustration 7). We aren't willing to risk failure unless the rewards far outweigh the risks. This approach is reasonable. However, we tend to carry this "emergency organ" approach too far even when the risk is not great; when the risk is only imagined to be great, we avoid creative action.

"Now I can be creative!"
Emergency Organ - The Mind
Illustration 7

The mayor of one of the largest cities in this country recently said, "It's a matter of survival for the city. We have not examined as closely as we could the city's operation. With the fiscal crunch, it now becomes critical to do so." This was in response to a city consultant's statement that, as one example of ways to save money, the city could handle sidewalk repairs with one-sixth the current manpower if certain changes in the approach to sidewalk repair were made. It took a financial crisis to stimulate this reevaluation of old ways of doing things and to risk the potential failure which accompanies efforts to try a new approach.

The prolific inventor, Charles Kettering, once stated that more educated people are _less_ likely to be good inventors. I don't agree with his statement completely. However, education does tend to teach us to conform; only to solve non-creative problems (those with the answer at the back of the book); to reward coming up with an idea and not taking the action required to implement our idea. It makes us trust written material such as books too much; leads us to believe that others who are more wise have the real answers; and separates learning from doing, which often results in an end to learning when we begin doing (working). Perhaps Kettering's remarks against education result-ed from the fact that our educational system leads us to believe that failure is wrong and of no value. However, as Dr. Land, inventor of the polaroid camera, remarked, "An essential aspect of creativity is not being afraid to fail." Scientists experiment and fail repeatedly before they get the results they want.

Need For One Answer Now!

I have assigned creative design problems to engineering students many times. The idea behind the creative design process, as I present-ed it to them, was to tackle an engineering design problem or invention creatively. They often developed good designs. However, invariably, the students presented preconceived designs before they had decided what to design. For example, the students were not willing to take the problem of how to invent a better mousetrap unless they already had an idea for a better mousetrap in their mind. In addition, it was very difficult to convince them to consider alternate solutions beyond their initial preconceived design.

Las Vegas is a good example of people's desire for immediate re-sults. Put your money down and in seconds you win or lose. This is much more exciting and attractive to many people than the delay of results which occurs if they invest their money. As a psychological counselor, I found that my greatest problem was to unlock my clients from erroneous preconceived solution to their problems. For example, a client might feel that his nervousness was due to his job. Often, this first idea as to the source of the problem was wrong. Perhaps his real problem was his marriage or finances. However, it was very difficult to get him to even consider alternate reasons for his problem.

When I taught college mathematics, I often offered several different approaches to solving a particular type of problem. Most students complained. They wanted one solution approach which works best all of the time. They didn't realize that the solution approach they liked best might be inappropriate for a slightly different kind of problem or for other students. My arguments to this end generally fell on the deaf ears of students. They would continue to try and convince me to present only a one-solution approach.

People don't want to suffer the anxiety of not having an immediate answer. When a problem is presented, we immediately offer a solution. Only if the first solution doesn't work will we consider trying another one.

Difficulty of Directed Mental Activity

Many of us find physical exertion easy but mental exertion difficult. We could improve our lives by thinking our goals through more carefully or budgeting our personal finances. However, we usually undertake tasks for long periods of time with little thinking. For example, we may play tennis for years. But during that time period, we may only briefly read or think about the strategies and skills required to play tennis. It would be nice if an empty head like an empty stomach would demand that it be filled and nourished. However, empty heads are often able to effectively block nourishment.

We often exert ourself mentally by worrying or wallowing in a hazy, messy cloud of thought out of which sometimes comes a thought of value. However, even then because we weren't looking for an answer to a problem, the idea or insight does not emerge from our mind. We often confuse how much thinking or worrying is done with how directed and productive it is.

Fear of Fun

It seems ludicrous that we might not be more creative because we might enjoy life more or have fun. However, sometimes people do feel guilty when they enjoy life or, as a professional, have that "how can I have fun when I am carrying the weight of the world on my shoulders" feeling.

Part of the process of creatively solving problems involves relaxation and playfulness intermixed with serious deliberations. Perhaps our inability to relax while solving problems is due to the magnitude of the problem we face or the insecurity we feel when facing any problem. People are often unaware that relaxation, fun and playfulness are important aspects of the creative problem-solving process.

Recognizing Good Solutions

An engineering manager observed that his company held weekly meetings to select design ideas to be developed by the company. Out of about 30 proposed ideas they would select and could afford to develop only a few. He felt that the selection process was very difficult and that the differences between the ideas selected and those rejected were very small.

It is virtually impossible to initially prove conclusively and objectively that one idea is better than another. Furthermore, one person's good solution to a problem, especially a personal problem may be a poor solution for someone else.

Therefore, because the mind is an emergency organ, it generally needs big immediate rewards to engage in action which offers only uncertain, inconclusive results. And if people cannot, as they have been educated to require in Western civilization, clearly and objectively find greater value in creative solutions when compared to habitual solutions, they may simply not be motivated enough to think up fresh, new ideas.

Criticism by Others

Unintentionally creativity is often retarded by the critical remarks of others (see illustration 8). When a new idea is introduced, it is often knocked down, kicked and beaten. The person with the idea is ridiculed with remarks like:

Wasn't that idea tried last year?

That's too radical.

It's a good idea, but the public isn't ready for it.

I'm glad you have the time to waste on that idea.

I just don't like it.

This just isn't the right time to try that.

Let someone else try it first.

Let's think about it for a while.

We never do it that way.

-38-

The Contribution of Others
Illustration 8

While reading these negative comments, you may have been saying to yourself, most creative ideas deserve those types of comments, and it's important to make them to help keep people in touch with reality. And to some extent you are right. The question is when and how these comments should be offered.

Summary

To become more creative, many obstacles must be overcome. It is impossible and unwise to try to overcome all obstacles to creative thinking. These same obstacles are also aids to everyday living. Without habits we would be perpetual beginners at everything we do--such as eating, driving and talking. Without fear of failure, we might fail too often. Without complacency, we might lack self-satisfaction, be anxious and restless. However, the fact that talent is abundant and desire is plentiful, creativity is rare, suggests that we need more creativity and less habit in our lives.

Creativity Grows with Exercise!

1. Estimate the percentage of your time each day devoted to conscious deliberate thinking. What percentage of your day should be devoted to thinking?

2. Estimate the percentage of your thinking devoted to coming up with new ideas.

3. Clasp your hands. Which thumb is on top? Try switching your clasp such that the opposite thumb is on top. How does that feel? Many times people say that it feels uncomfortable. List as many reasons as you can why a person might find this change uncomfortable.

4. Ask three people what two obstacles they face when trying to be more creative. Discuss their comments.

5. Discuss the possible negative impact on a person's life which might result from not using creativity often enough.

6. Discuss the negative impact on a person's life which might result if one is creative too often.

7. What are some ways we might overcome

   a. our fear of failure?

   b. our complacency?

   c. our tendency to initially consider only one solution for each problem?

8. A farmer had some land which was to be divided equally among his

four children into four parcels. His land is shown below:

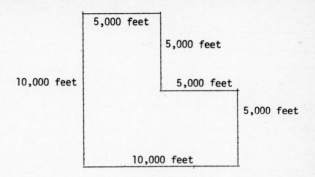

The parcels must be of the same size and shape. Try to draw the parcels on the above figure. A solution is at the end of these exercises.

9. List as many reasons as you can why solving problem 8 is difficult. What obstacles did you encounter when you tried to solve this problem?

10. What are some possible reasons why mental work is so much harder for us to do than physical work?

11. Which five habits of yours most restrict your creativity?

12. What steps can you take to overcome those habits you listed for exercise 11?

13. For the next week try to change a simple but frequently used habit and report your experience. For example, you might try to brush your teeth with the opposite hand.

Solution to problem 8:

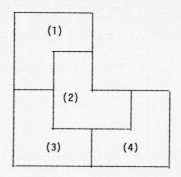

Chapter 4

CREATIVE PEOPLE AS PROBLEM SOLVERS

The picture of the creative person painted in this book is a composite of the creative problem-solving characteristics of successful, creative people such as Frank Lloyd Wright, Robert Frost and Albert Einstein who exhibited creativity at a fairly high rate. Many similarities in their approaches to creative problem solving exist. However, many more variations are found in their approaches than similarities when any particular creative person is examined. Like businessmen or athletes, creative people have many characteristics in common yet exhibit many individual differences. These creative attributes may help you develop your own creative ability.

Problem-Solving Characteristics

Creative people have a higher motivation to, and capability for, recognizing valuable problems. They are able to bring to a clear focus the exact nature of a problem and engage their conscious and unconscious minds to solve it. They are receptive to their own new ideas and those of other people. They combine judgment and intuition based on their knowledge and experience to select the best solutions. And they have the energy and commitment necessary to transform their ideas into usable results.

Recognizing Valuable Problems. Creative people choose a single, specific life focus; a particular type of activity, profession or interest. It may be art, athletics, science, or cooking. As psychologist Frank Barron wrote, in Creativity and Personal Freedom, "Even regularly original persons can be expected to be outstanding only one or two ways." They are knowledgeable of the current status of their field and aware and sensitive to shortcomings, needs and opportunities within it. They are easily aroused and challenged by missing elements, inconsistencies and omissions.

Creative people can live with the uncertainty of not knowing all the answers. They are more concerned about improving their field of interest than favorably impressing others. They seek to organize their experience and ideas and bring meaning into them.

Defining the Real Problems. The experience and inner sensitivity of creative people helps them select problems which are not so awesome that a solution is impossible, yet not so easy that the solution is obvious or of little value. The problems pursued by creative people are usually complex and undefined. They rely on the depth of their knowledge, intuition and feeling to help define the problem. They identify the "real" problem--not just a symptom or superficial aspect of a problem.

Opening to Inner and Outer Ideas for Solutions. Creative people have a complexity of outlook, an adventurousness of mind and an independence of judgment which allows them to consider many possible solutions from many diverse sources. They are capable of drawing divergent thoughts and hints for the solution to their problems from their innerself, other people and their environment. They are tolerant of the ambiguity in their problem and ideas for its solution. And they are tolerant of, and will play with partial, incomplete and sometimes foolish ideas recognizing that a poor or partial idea may lead to another better one. They can live with the anxiety of not having an immediate answer for long periods of time.

Using Judgment and Intuition to Identify Solutions. Creative people trust their feelings, their unconscious thoughts, in addition to their conscious, deliberate, step-by-step, systematic thinking. They are able to wait until a solution arrives which feels right and is logically right. They rely on their unconscious mind to help select the final solution to the problem. Because of the importance of unconscious problem solving, it will be treated more fully in the second half of this chapter.

Transforming Solutions into Usable Results. Initial ideas, obtained from the incubation process or conscious, deliberate thinking, are usually rough and underdeveloped. They must be modified, clarified and simplified to be usable solutions. The creative person has the strength and persistence necessary to perform this often laborious task.

Creative people also have the courage and self-confidence necessary to put their solution into practice. They face frustration as a challenge to their creativity. They proceed in spite of criticism of their ideas and yet are open enough to modify or drop them if the criticism is valid.

If they fail, they are able to learn from their failure and try again. They recognize the high risk of making mistakes which is inherent in tackling difficult new problems. They can't tolerate being bored by life and are continually trying to improve it. They are more concerned about what they think of themselves than what others think of them.

They are willing to work hard. It is possible that no one works harder in our society than the inventor, artist, scientist or composer. Years of concentrated work spent bringing a solution to a successful conclusion is often a characteristic of the creative person.

Because this description of the creative person as a problem solver fits no person completely, many people may use it as an excuse not to be creative. However, some very creative people are good at recognizing opportunities and some are good at implementing ideas. There are no all-around creative people. On the other hand, we all have creative potential in some areas of creative problem solving and can develop others.

Many of us have a defect such as poor spelling or being inarticulate and let that stop us from utilizing our creativity. Handicaps didn't stop Yeats and Shaw who were poor spellers; Einstein, Poe and Roentgen who were expelled from school; Franklin, Picasso and Adler who were poor at mathematics; or Edison who was at the bottom of his class in school. Physical handicaps aren't an excuse either. Louis Pasteur made many great discoveries after he had a stroke which destroyed half of his brain. Therefore, recognize that you aren't the "all-around" creative person but that you do have the opportunity to develop what creativity you possess and to make a contribution to society.

Unconscious Thinking

Unconscious thinking occurs below the level of awareness and is generally unavailable to the aware or conscious mind even when an effort is made to make it aware. Creative ideas which come unexpectedly from unconscious thinking are said to have incubated.

The illuminations, sudden insights and Eureka experiences experienced by most creative people are generally attributed to incubation. A famous incident of incubation occurred in the third century B.C. in

Sicily. King Hiero suspected that his goldsmith had used some silver instead of all gold to make his royal crown. The king asked the mathematician Archimedes to determine if this was true.

Archimedes struggled with the problem for a long period of time. Then, while taking a bath, he <u>suddenly</u> noticed that his body caused some water to spill over (see illustration 9). In an instant, he realized the solution to the problem. To determine the truth, he would see if the king's crown displaced as much water as a similar amount of pure gold. Whereupon he jumped out of the tub in the public baths and ran home naked, shouting as he ran: "Eureka! Eureka! I've found it! I've found it!"

Production of dramatically new ideas by a process of purely conscious calculation rarely seems to occur. Unconscious thinking, thinking which you are unaware of, is a major contributor to the production of new ideas. It is used in every field of endeavor. Artists, such as Blake, Emerson and Shelley, have used it. Inventors, Edison and Kettering, used it. Great thinkers, such as Nietzsche and Gauss, used it. Shakespeare called it "the spell in which imagination bodies forth the forms of things unknown."

Incubation
Illustration 9

The poet, Amy Lowell, revealed that an idea would come into her mind for no apparent reason. For instance, she once thought that horses would be a good subject for a poem. After this initial thought, she had no more conscious thought about it. But what she had really done was to drop her subject into the unconscious, "much as one drops a letter into the mailbox." Six months later, the words of the poem began to come into her head, the poem - to use her private vocabulary - "was there."

Walt Disney suffered from insomnia. Many of his ideas dropped into his mind during sleepless nights. He used to arrive at work in the morning with more ideas than anyone could use. The mathematician, Henri Poincaré, reported that the role of the unconscious in mathematical invention is "incontestable." Albert Einstein got many of his best ideas in the morning while shaving.

James Watt's condenser for the Newcomen steam engine was one of the greatest inventions of modern times and it opened the way for the general application of steam power. He had worked unsuccessfully on this problem for two years. Then, "on a fine Sabbath afternoon," during a walk, his unconscious thinking brought the answer into awareness. Watt reported,

"I had entered the green and had passed the old washing house. I was thinking of the engine at the time. I had gone as far as the herd's house when the idea came into my mind that as steam was an elastic body it would rush into a vacuuum, and if a connection were made between the cylinder and exhausting vessel it would rush into it and might then be condensed without cooling the cylinder . . . . I had not walked further than the Golf house when the whole thing was arranged in my mind."

Even the courts are beginning to recognize the concept of the unconscious mind. George Harrison of the Beatles singing group was found guilty of plagiarism of the 1962 John Mack hit tune, "He's so Fine," for his own 1970 hit record, "My Sweet Lord." The judge concluded that Harrison did not plagiarize deliberately. According to the judge, "His unconsciousness knew that song had worked out, but his conscious mind did not remember."

Ordinary talent produces artistically and creatively by rational selection and combination guided primarily by conscious thinking. It may accomplish something excellent, but can never attain anything great. Creative genius comes from the unconscious. It's as if the "ordinary" person's conscious mind were ignorant of the unconscious mind and its capabilities, or as if "ordinary" persons' conscious minds actually mistrusted the unconscious. Creative people tend to trust and capitalize on the unconscious.

The conscious mind is like the tip of an iceberg. It is the part observable and represents only a very small portion of the vastness of the mind. The remaining unconscious mind is hidden by the surface of the water in our memory. The tip of the iceberg is kept afloat by the ice below the water just as the unconscious mind keeps the conscious mind afloat with ideas. The unconscious mind is continuously thinking and solving problems.

Freud believed that every idea begins in the unconscious. It becomes conscious according to the level of resistance it meets by the mental "censor or filter." If the idea is found to be acceptable and safe by the "censor," it becomes conscious.

The Unconscious as an Aid to Problem Solving. It is possible to direct the unconscious mind. Archimedes did not obtain his Eureka experience by chance. As Pasteur said, "Chance favors only the prepared mind." Archimedes got his idea by "chance" because he had first worked hard on the problem and engaged his mind to it; worried and thought about it. He focused the energy of his unconscious on the problem. The unconscious then helped to solve the problem. Archimedes' relaxed mental silence allowed the solution to pop into his conscious mind.

To derive maximum benefit from the unconscious as an aid to conscious problem solving, we need to focus our attention and energy on a specific problem or goal which is important to us. Then, we should carefully define the problem and try to solve it consciously to help engage our unconscious mind.

Working on a problem daily and working on only one major problem at a time can help us focus and engage the unconscious mind. Many people have engaged the unconscious by writing down their problem or problems several times each morning.

After you have worked on the problem and engaged your mind, incubate. Quiet the mind. Think, calculate, worry, judge, try, hope and control _less_. Take a break. Relax. Sleep on it. Think of other things. Jog. Take a shower. Take a car ride. Do anything that relaxes you and takes your mind off the problem. Ideas do not come by just relaxing. They come from the areas where you have first focused intensive conscious mental activity and thereby initiated and engaged your unconscious thinking energy. The person relaxing in illustration 10 may be rewarded with a sudden insight or Eureka experience if his previous conscious, deliberate thinking has sufficiently engaged the unconscious mind.

Relaxing to Create
Illustration 10

When we are relaxed, we are more in contact with our unconscious thought and increase our creativity. Research has shown that people think more creatively relaxed and lying down than while standing up. Recent studies indicate that, as with sports, creative thinking occurs best when we are able to enter a state of relaxed attention.

Alpha brain wave activity is associated with relaxation. According to C. J. Martindale, when creative people go to work on an imaginative task, their alpha waves increase. "Most people produce alpha waves when they are relaxing, and reduce alpha frequency when they are working on a problem."[1]

Freud felt that dreams often provided hints to the unconscious thoughts. Wagner, Coleridge, and Beethoven attributed dreams as a source of some of their great creative ideas.

Aldous Huxley observed an everyday experience, "Everyone is familiar with the experience of forgetting a name, straining to capture it and ignominiously failing. Then, if one is wise, one will stop trying to remember and allow the mind to sink into a condition of alert passivity. The chances are that the name will come bobbing up into consciousness of its own accord. Memory works best, it would seem, when the mind is in a state of dynamic relaxation."

Most of us have experienced a similar memory enhancement when tension is released. We have walked out of a test and remembered something we could not remember during the test or, when we are more relaxed after an argument, we have remembered a key point that we wish we would have

---

[1] C. J. Martindale, "Creative People: What Makes Them So Different," Psychology Today, July 1975, pp. 44-50.

made during the argument. Perhaps the practice of counting to ten before acting when we are mad is an approach to using the reason encapsulated in our unconscious mind to soften the irrationality of our conscious mind.

Meditation and relaxation are ways to allow unconscious ideas to penetrate the conscious. Maharishi Yogi calls Transcendental Meditation the science of creative intelligence. Relaxation and meditation do tap the unconscious in a random, unforced, undirected fashion. However, they do not focus your energy on solving a particular problem.

Writers get written out, scientists, in effect, experimented out, and artists, in effect, drawn out. They run out of ideas, energy, patience, concentration and freshness. This is an appropriate and meaningful time to stop "beating your mind against a stone wall" and relax, sleep on it, take a mental vacation, incubate or change direction. Your unconscious mind may provide you with a new idea during this time period. As a minimum you will come back to the problem with a fresh mind and new determination.

People engaged in brainstorming sessions have reportedly generated their most creative ideas after "sleeping on it." That is, working hard on a problem one day, then resuming their work on it the next day.

Sometimes conscious mental activity interferes with the automatic more powerful unconscious activity. D. T. Suguki, the renowned Zen master, describes this type of interference in Zen in the Art of Archery:

"As soon as we reflect, deliberate, and conceptualize, the original unconsciousness is lost and a thought interferes... The arrow is off the string but does not fly straight to the target, nor does the target stand where it is. Calculation, which is miscalculation, sets in..."

When Ideas Incubate. Conditions of insomnia and the state between wakefulness and sleep are common times for creative insights. I often have my best insights during this time period. As mentioned earlier, Walt Disney got many of his ideas during insomniac nights.

The sudden insight resulting from incubation can occur at any time in the middle of the night, at church, while shaving or loafing on the beach. Be ready to catch the incubated ideas. Most creative people report having experienced good ideas coming from incubation, and most creative people have reported forgetting good ideas or insights because they didn't write them down. Many creative ideas become lost in our own minds. So be prepared. Have a paper and pencil readily available, wherever you are. Preferably, you should carry some paper and pen or pencil around with you. My friend scientist-inventor, Doug Nash, reported that many of his creative ideas drop into his mind while he is driving on the freeway. Emerson took time out each day for meditating quietly before brooks.

The insight or idea can reveal itself to your conscious mind immediately or after hours, days, years or never. Therefore, often due to deadlines, we must make a conscious decision before our unconscious mind reveals the best decision to us.

My first corporate client, who was using creative problem solving skills to help facilitate a group of his employees who were trying to solve an important problem, kept asking when the best solution idea would come and how he would recognize it. I assured him that it would come soon and arise from the unconscious and would be obvious to him. He got more

-54-

impatient after each weekly session. I was getting nervous recognizing that a great idea might never come. Luckily, during the last scheduled session, the executive had an "aha," "Eureka," type experience. He excitedly exclaimed, "I've got it - this is the answer!"

What Incubates? The sudden flash, aha or Eureka experience is sometimes a complete finished idea or insight but more often it is a result of incomplete and many times inaccurate insights or ideas. They are often brief, flabby, rough, and untamed. It's the conscious mind's job to expand on, clarify and modify the rough idea seed. The creative person must use his vast reservoir of knowledge and experience to polish and refine the idea.

Summary

William James once said that we learn to swim in the winter and to skate in the summer. Unconscious mental activity which incubates ideas is a powerful resource for all people, especially people who learn to capitalize on it. Most creative people do. Resultant ideas generally meet the conscious during periods of relaxation or during the transition between work and relaxation. They are usually of maximum value if we have just focused our energies and engaged our minds to work on a particular problem.

Take advantage of your unconscious. Make it an integral part of your deliberate problem solving efforts. Perhaps it's because man wants to be consciously in control of things that we don't utilize the unconscious more. Educators often never mention it or try to integrate it into their pedagogical schemes even though it is the most often cited source of great, creative ideas.

Don't run down to relax on the beach, sit all day in the bathtub or watch a brook expecting to experience a creative idea or insight, unless you first prepare by researching the problem and engage your mind to the problem. A dentist I know of does this by simply writing down a couple of problems each morning and then consciously forgetting about them. Usually at least one is solved during the day. His problems are small compared with those tackled by Einstein and other great thinkers. Nevertheless, he does take advantage of his unconscious. I have had success with writing down one problem several different ways for about one minute each morning. Later in the day, without any conscious effort on my part, a satisfactory solution pops into my mind from my subconscious. Try some of the exercises which follow. They may work for you.

To be able to utilize the unconscious mind effectively, we need to recognize important problems to feed the unconscious; carefully define these problems to engage the unconscious mind; think clearly and deliberately; and work hard to transform the rough ideas which the unconscious incubates into workable usable ideas.

Creativity Grows with Exercise!

1. Carry a pen and some 3 x 5 cards around with you all day and place them near your bed at night for twenty-four hours. Record any ideas or fresh insights which you have and what you are doing when the insights occur. Discuss the results.

2. Focus on a problem. Write down a problem whose solution would be of value to you. For example: In what ways can I improve my verbal communication skills? List any ideas that immediately come to your mind. Then, for two days, state the problem to yourself over and over again for about one minute each morning.

Record any ideas which incubate. Discuss the results.

3. This exercise is reserved for the truly adventurous people. Use some method of keeping yourself in the twilight zone between being asleep and awake. Enter that state for about one hour and record ideas that incubate. Walt Disney came up with many of his best ideas during nights of insomnia. Discuss the results.

Possible methods of keeping yourself in the twilight zone:

1) Eat something disagreeable that will keep you from falling asleep immediately at night.

2) Try to take a nap. However, have an annoying buzzer ringing every ten minutes.

3) Lie on your back on a hard surface and try to fall asleep holding a can up with one arm bent at the elbow. If you fall asleep, the can will fall and wake you up.

4) Sleep with shoes or clothes on.

4. Ask three people you know if they have experienced sudden insights or ideas dropping into their mind during periods of rest or relaxation. If they did, ask about the circumstances surrounding their incubated gift. Discuss the results.

5. Describe an ideal "creative thinking" room which would help you be more creative.

Chapter 5

DELIBERATE CREATIVITY

Most of our thinking may be likened to a cloud blown about and shaped by its environment, occasionally forming clearly defined images or ideas, but most of the time it drifts uneventfully. Sometimes it is stormy and stressful and sometimes calm and restful.

Occasionally our mind will absorb knowledge as a cloud does moisture. If the amount and kind of knowledge are sufficient, creative ideas will rain down and may fall on productive soil. Or the cloud may dissipate and release no moisture.

Conscious, deliberate, creative processes and methods strive to guide the formation, form and flow of the mind. They seed the mind and catalyze the formation of new ideas and fresh insights. They direct the precipitation of solution ideas onto fertile problems, problems whose solutions are of value to the individual and/or society.

If someone says "I can't think creatively," the major difficulty may actually lie in making contact with their natural creativity which is an important part of each of us. They probably lack the skill and art of directing their creative ideas onto fertile ground and thereby making it productive.

In some of us, creativity "just happens." We have sudden insights and illumination. This accidental creativity oftentimes does not form quickly enough to meet the needs and deadlines of our dynamically changing lives. The thrust of deliberate creative thinking methods is to stimulate, direct, strengthen, guide, accelerate and make timely our natural creativity so that it is available when we want it, so that fresh insights and new ideas of value will result. Alex F. Osborn, the father of brainstorming, observed that "Just as we can throttle our imagination, we can likewise accelerate it."

In his book, <u>Eupsychian Management</u>, Abraham H. Maslow observed that "We are involved here in the paradox that there must be a transition between being something bad and being something good. If a thief becomes conscious of the fact that he is a thief and wants to become an honest man instead, there is no way in which he can do this except by consciously trying not to be a thief and consciously trying to be an honest man. Trying to be an honest man is self-conscious, artificial, not spontaneous honesty which is an expression of deep-lying character attitudes. And yet, what else is possible? There is no other way to jump from being a crook to being an honest man except by trying." Deliberate creative techniques, strategies, catalysts, and prompters are not as powerful as natural creativity. However, if our present nature does not involve sufficient creativity and we want to become more creative, like the thief who wants to become an honest man, we must consciously and deliberately try. Even though we may be artificial, self-consciously spontaneous, not natural and may look like a phony in the process, no other alternative exists for this desired change.

Dr. Norbert Weiner once stated that man cannot even perform such a simple operation as picking up a cigarette from a table by conscious thought or "will." When you consciously try to hit a tennis ball using new and perhaps ultimately better strokes, you usually fail at first. However, with continued trials, having the new stroke firmly in mind, you are usually able to master the stroke, and it becomes a part of your "natural" tennis game.

"Psychologists sometimes raise the question of whether learning specific methods of solving problems may create 'sets' or fixed habits that interfere with a way of solving a particular problem. It is precisely against any such rigidity--such interference with flexible associations--that programs to nurture creative ability are designed. In a sense, an effective program attempts to establish habits against habits (a set against set) when approacning new situations, yet ones which will allow a person to live with certain temporary sets or habits required in our society. Here the individual will want to recognize that these temporary ones are deliberate sets as opposed to 'blind sets.'"[1]

The creative methods discussed now, and the DO-IT process discussed later, are at first forced and unnatural but eventually bring us closer to a natural way of being and creating rather than further away. The forces in our environment and our conscious mind have tended to distort our natural creativity. Deliberate creativity offers a useful path back to natural creativity.

Deliberate creative techniques are designed to help overcome obstacles to creativity. They help us focus our energies on one problem at a time so that we are not overwhelmed by problems. They help protect us from failure at certain times during the creative problem-solving process. They help us transform failure into growth. They help us capitalize on our emotions and the holistic side of our brain. They help us tap our unconscious mind. They help us teach the value of delaying judgment and seeking many ideas. They make us become more

[1]Sidney J. Parnes, _Creative Behavior Guidebook_. New York; Scribner's Sons, 1967, pp. 20-21.

comfortable with mental thinking, provide periods of relaxation and fun during the problem solving process to help release good ideas. By using these processes, we not only get fresh insights and new ideas, we increase our natural creativity as well.

We are all problem solvers. Some may not consider art to be a problem solving profession. However, one artist wrote that there are many problems that beset the artist in his work. Consciously or unconsciously each artist tries to solve them. He said, "Lately I have come to the stage where I _actually_ take an art problem and try to solve it. For example, I was interested in painting a dark object within the dark. In order to carry this out successfully, it may take me several years. Once accomplished to my satisfaction, however, it becomes an integral part of me, enabling me to go on to another problem." Not only do artists solve problems, but this particular artist has learned to consciously, deliberately solve problems.

In this chapter several established creative techniques are presented. In Part II of this text new techniques are presented. No one technique is correct or best for everyone all of the time. Experiment with them, select those which work best for you. Modify them to meet your personal needs and utilize your personal strengths. None of these methods are perfect. However, unless you are satisfied with your present level of creativity, they offer you one way of becoming more creative. Even if the use of techniques only makes a small step forward in your effort to become more creative, it is a very important step and can be the beginning of many more steps.

Quantity of Ideas

Creative techniques to varying degrees all rely on first developing many ideas as a way to obtain good, creative ideas. The human tendency to grasp the first idea, solution or explanation that comes to mind and cling to it is a major detriment to creativity. If the problem is a minor one, such as what will I have for lunch, this approach may be appropriate. However, if it is a major problem where we want to obtain new and original solutions, we need many ideas to choose from--the more the better. John F. Kennedy revealed his concern about limited choices on a national scale by saying, "We intended to have a wider choice than humiliation or all-out nuclear war."

Once we have our first immediate solution, we have it forever. Then we can proceed to look for new and better alternative solutions. If we don't find any better ones, we can always return to the original one. If we want to get a truly good apple, we don't take the first one we pick up--we examine many apples to get the best one (see illustration 11). To select a beauty queen, a representative for the Olympics or an academic scholarship recipient, many applicants are first considered. In general, the more that are considered, the better is the chance of obtaining an outstanding one.

If you want a good apple, select from a
large number of apples!

Quality from Quantity
Illustration 11

Edison constructed three thousand different ideas in connection
with the electric light, each of them reasonable and apparently likely
to be good.   Yet in only two cases did his experiments prove the truth
of his theory and lead to patents.   He once said he would try anything
to solve a technical problem even Limburger cheese.

Charles F. Kettering remarked that to develop a new diesel engine
he tried one thing after another for about six years until he found an
answer.   Artists and cartoonists usually draw many, many initial sketches
before they pursue one to a finished product.   Van Gogh wrote that he
drew repeatedly until there was one drawing that was different from the
rest, one which didn't look like an ordinary drawing.

The Pacific Telephone Company made twenty-five takes in the studio
of a 7 1/2 second recording which it planned to use as one of its recorded messages.   They wanted the tape to project both warmth and authority.   Every syllable was planned.   The person recorded was a

professional speaker and a member of the American Federation of Television and Radio Artists. Yet, because the message recorded was important and would be heard by up to two million people daily, twenty-five takes were made before the best one was selected.

Research has confirmed the fact that out of many ideas come good creative ideas. The research findings indicate that the ideas produced toward the end of an idea generating session contain more good, creative ideas. The initial ideas stimulate, trigger and provide ideas for later ideas. They help release ideas from the unconscious mind. Having lots of ideas tends to lead to diversity as well as originality in ideas because as we run out of ideas we are forced into fresh new approaches.

Alfred North Whitehead provided good insight into the value of quantity with these words, "We need to entertain every prospect of novelty, every chance that could result in new combinations, and subject them to the most impartial scrutiny. For the probability is that nine hundred and ninety-nine of them will come to nothing, either because they are worthless in themselves or because we shall not know how to elicit their value; but we had better entertain them all however skeptically, for the thousandth idea may be the one that will change the world."

The master detectives Sherlock Holmes and Ellery Queen always begin their investigations with an open mind about "who done it." In illustration 12, Sherlock observes many possible causes of the apparent death, even when the cause of death appears to be obvious.

Sherlock and Quantity
Illustration 12

Eugene Von Fange presented the case for using quantity to get quality as well in his book, _Professional Creativity_. He wrote, "A pearl diver goes out in his boat to the oyster beds, takes off his clothes, dons his swim suit and helmet, tosses a bag over his shoulder, and dives into the water. He very efficiently collects oysters and, when the bed is exhausted, he surfaces, goes ashore, and opens each one. Certainly, he would not hunt around until he found one oyster, then surface, climb into his boat, take off his paraphernalia, put on his clothes, take out his knife, break open the oyster, search for a pearl, and, if none were found, repeat the entire process with another oyster."

Yet, foolish as it is, this is just the way most of us try to get ideas. We insist upon dropping our established judicial filter the instant it receives one idea "oyster" from our imagination. We climb into our evaluative clothes to tear the idea to pieces, looking for some speck of a pearl before we go after another oyster. In brainstorm sessions we are looking only for oysters. We want to accumulate them all before we begin to make an efficient appraisal of them.

We can experience diversity coming from quantity by trying the following exercise. List as many birds as you can! Try to list at least 25 different birds. Don't read further - try it! Most people start out by listing birds like sparrows, robins and canaries. As they run out of these kinds of birds, their stretch for quantity often forces them into naming a new category of bird like a turkey, which in turn leads to chicken, duck and goose. Further stretch for quantity may lead to hawk which will in turn lead to eagle, owl and falcon. Once we begin on a track of ideas with similar characteristics such as duck and chicken, we tend to be locked into that chain of thought. When we run out of ideas, if we are forcing ourselves to strive for quantity we may break into a new track leading us in a divergent direction and many new possible ideas.

Obtaining a title for this book was important. The following list of possible titles are some of those I considered before selecting the final title. Even though I still may have not obtained the best title, selecting from many titles is more likely to lead to a good title than if only a few titles were considered. Titles considered included:

"A Practical Guide to the Art of Creatively Solving Problems," "An Experience in Creative Thinking," "DO IT Creatively," "Introduction to DO IT," "A Practical Process for Creative Problem Solving," "The Creative Way," "Guideposts for Doing It Creatively," "Pleasure and

Creativity," "Mind Liberation," "The Act of Creative Thinking," "Becoming More Creative," "Creatively Solving Creative Problems," "Unfolding Your Creative Blossom," "The Nourishment, Care and Unfolding of Your Creativity," "Creative Problem Solving," "Deliberate Creativity," "Brain Dusting," "Everyone Can Be Creative," "Mind Expanding," "Creativity Acceleration," "How to Become More Creative," "Creative Catalysts," "Workbook on Creativity," "Focused Creativity," "Realistic Creative Problem Solving," "Conscious Thinking," "Focused Thinking," and "A Process for Creativity."

The importance of quantity as central to creativity is underscored by the approach psychologists use to measure or test our creativity. Most tests designed to measure our creativity use problems which measure our ability to develop many diverse ideas as a central indication of creativity. They may ask us to list as many ideas as we can for the use of a brick or coat hanger. Our creativity score is determined to a great extent by the quantity and diversity of the ideas we list.

A seven year old girl was trying to design a picture for a neighborhood art contest. The rules of the contest were that the child was to be the sole designer of the art work. Her father's way of indirectly helping her was to provide her with a large variety of materials such as rocks, cotton, cloth and paper to choose from. It helped. She won a prize. She was able to obtain a quality idea from the many possible combinations presented to her.

Most people, industries and government do use quantity to get quality. However, they use it by accident, unintentionally and haphazardly. If they have a problem they soon have one solution which they try; if it fails, they try another. If that idea fails, they try more until they meet success. The creative way is to first consider many possible solutions. Then select one or two. Try them. If they don't work, modify them or try the next best idea, and so on. This accidental, "forced by failure to use of many ideas" has many drawbacks. A poor initial solution may work and therefore be used. Even after many trials, much expense and time is exerted, only an average solution may be instituted.

One of the obstacles to getting lots of ideas is that we tend to want only good safe ideas. However, most often good ideas come only after inadequate ones have been generated and considered. These poor ideas often lay the groundwork for or prompt the good ideas. Psychologist Dr. J. P. Guilford has stated that the person who is capable of producing a large number of ideas per unit of time, other things being equal, has a greater chance of having significant ideas.

At the heart of getting creative ideas is producing a large number of ideas, even poor and wild ideas, which lead to diversity, originality, many choices and finally the best idea. "No idea is so outlandish that it should not be considered," said Winston Churchill. Incubation, delaying judgment, brainstorming, checklists and synectics are in effect tools for obtaining large numbers of ideas. The central tenant of brainstorming and most creative methods is to seek quantity and diversity. To become more creative, you must be willing to generate more ideas than you can use. "The best way to have a good idea is to have lots of ideas," wrote Nobel Prize-winning scientist Linus Pauling.

Brainstorming

The brainstorming technique is probably the most widely used and poorly understood creative problem solving technique. Many people use the term brainstorming to refer to _any_ process that generates a new idea. Or they use it to refer to any group problem-solving process.

Actually, the brainstorming technique is an idea-generating activity which attempts to overcome obstacles to creativity by stressing the deferment of judgment and criticism. It encourages many ideas including far out, wild and silly ideas with the hope that they may lead to good creative ideas. This approach tends to produce new original ideas in addition to conventional ones.

The concept of delaying judgment is central to brainstorming. Dr. S. Parnes, Director of the Creative Education Foundation, likens allowing yourself to be critical at the same time you are being creative to trying to get hot and cold water from the same faucet at the same time. The ideas aren't hot enough and the criticism isn't cold enough. The results are tepid. The essential rules for brainstorming are:

1. Delay judgment. Don't criticize or evaluate ideas while the brain-storming session is in progress. Choose the best ideas after many ideas have been developed.

2. Strive for a large number of ideas. List as many ideas as you can. List them as fast as you can. Use far-out laughable ideas to try to stimulate conventional ideas.

Brainstorming is usually considered to be a group problem solving technique, capitalizing on the fact that ideas from one person stimulate ideas in others. However, it can be practiced on an individual basis.

Alex F. Osborn is generally credited with the origination, development and early promotion of brainstorming. His book, Applied Imagi-nation, focuses on the brainstorming techniques. It is written in lay terms and includes many examples.

Synectics

Analogies have long been used as an aid to the creative design process. Synectics is a highly developed method or process which uses metaphors and analogies to generate creative ideas and fresh insights into problems. To break from previous habits and old ideas and to introduce relaxing "vacations" into the process, the synectics process tries to "make the familiar strange" and the "strange familiar."

A brief example of the synectics problem solving approach applied to the problem of re-examining an existing corporate organization structure follows: To "make the familiar strange," we will use a box of matches to represent or be analogous to an organizational structure. Next we list the attributes of the match box, forgetting about the original problem for a moment. A box of matches has six sides, it includes a center section which slides in and out. It is made of cardboard and has a striking surface on two sides. Next we try to "make the strange familiar." We try to "force" the attributes of the match box to be like those of the organization and structure we are examining. The striking surface may be likened to the protection an organization needs from strikes. The sliding insert may stimulate the idea that the heart of an organization should be slidable or flexible. The six sides may represent six essential organization divisions. Thus, we have used the analogy of a match box to force some fresher insights into the design of a corporate organization.

This example of synectics does not give justice to the depth and complexity of the synectics process. For example, the above match box example is considered by synectics theory to be direct analogy. Fantasy and personal analogies are also used by the experienced practitioner of the synectics art to stimulate creative ideas. The synectics method is treated fully in _Synectics_, by W. J. J. Gordon and _The Practice of Creativity_, by Gordon M. Prince.

Goal Focusing

Dr. Maxwell Maltz, in his book _Psycho Cybernetics_, described his method of creatively achieving desired future results. It consists of experiencing through your imagination the formation of new automatic reaction patterns by "acting as if" something you desire to occur in the future were now true.

For example, say you want to become president of the company in which you work. For a few minutes each morning you should relax, close your eyes and visualize in detail, using your imagination, yourself as _already_ being president. The daily effort tends to focus your mind on that goal and engages its "automatic servo-mechanism" toward that direction. In time, according to Dr. Maltz, you may either attain the presidency or at least progress closer to it.

Checklists

Checklists or idea needler lists are often used as a technique to stimulate new ideas and to make sure you have considered standard engineering design considerations. A sample checklist like ones often used by value engineers follows:

1. Is it needed?

2. Does it cost more than it's worth?

3. Can something else do the job better?

4. Does it do more than is necessary? Can some of its features be eliminated without impairing function?

5. Can its function or parts be combined?

6. Can a standard product be found which will be usable?

7. If it was your money, would you refuse to buy the item because it cost too much?

8. Why does it have this shape?

9. What if this were larger? Higher? Longer? Wider? Thicker? Lower?

10. How can it appeal to the senses?

11. How about adding more value?

12. What if this were made bigger?

13. How can this be made more compact?

14. Would this be better symmetrical or asymmetrical?

15. In what form could this be?

16. Can motion be added to it?

17. Will it be better standing still?

18. Has a search been made of the patent literature? Trade journals?

19. How could this be made easier to use?

20. Can it be made safer?

Methods Used at Hot Point Company of Focusing Creativity

Methods used by the Hot Point Company to improve their productivity include the "Waste - not - method," the "And - also" method and the "Tear - down - method."

The "Waste - not - method" focuses creative energies on how to prevent wasting anything. For example, if a small packing box is being thrown away, creative efforts would be focused on ways of using all or part of the otherwise discarded box.

The "And - also - method" is a technique which exaggerates the strategy of delaying judgment. Instead of criticizing an idea or a product, you assume it is good and try and make it better. You, in effect, try to say yes to the current design or preliminary idea and add ideas or modifications saying, "This will make it even better."

The "Tear - down - technique" is used to improve products by first thinking up all possible limitations and/or failings of a specific product; then, trying to correct its failings and deficiencies.

Procter and Gamble's Elimination Approach

Procter and Gamble uses teams of employees to try to eliminate existing things and unnecessary things which are planned for the future. Nothing is sacred, and effort is made to eliminate all things. Generally, major cost items are attacked first. However, often good results are obtained by trying to eliminate even low cost items.

For example, they attacked the need for light switches in a planned warehouse. It turned out that if lights were left burning all the time, the cost would be about $300 a year. Switches to turn them off when the lights weren't needed might save about $150 per year in energy costs. The switches would cost $7,200. A mathematical analysis revealed that it would take almost 50 years in energy money saved by installing the switches to pay for the switches. So they eliminated the switches from the warehouse plans.

Their creative teams often focus on three questions:

1. Can it be eliminated completely?

2. Can it be eliminated partially?

3. Is there a lower-cost alternative?

Delaying Judgment

Each of the deliberate creativity techniques discussed require that we delay judgment on initial, preliminary ideas. Edison's experiments in electric lighting were protested by the president of a major university who said that everyone acquainted with the subject well-recognized these experiments as conscious fallacies. The first successful cast iron plow invented in 1797 was rejected by New Jersey farmers under the theory that cast iron poisoned the land and stimulated the growth of weeds. Examples of erroneous quick judgments on new ideas abound. On the other hand, without judging or criticizing ideas, we could not select the best ones and our resources would be squandered indiscriminately.

Our thinking mind tends to be two-fold: judicial-analyzing, comparing, and choosing and creative-building, visualizing, foreseeing and generating ideas. Judgment can help keep imagination on the track. Imagination can help stimulate and enlighten judgment. William James, the psychologist, wrote that "First a new theory is attacked as absurd; then it is admitted to be true, but obvious and insignificant; finally it is seen to be so important that its adversaries claim they themselves discovered it."

Everyone excels in judging and criticizing. Typically when an original idea is offered, one person knocks it to the ground. Another kicks its. Another spits on it. If it tries to rise and show that it might be a good idea, someone else knocks it down again.

That idea was thought of 50 years ago!

We don't have enough time or money for it!

This isn't the right time for that idea!

It will never work!

We never do it that way!

I just don't like it!

There is a place for criticism in problem solving. However, we should give an idea a chance. Judging or criticizing ideas while generating ideas gets you nowhere. It's like stepping on the gas pedal while you have your other foot on the brake. You get nowhere!

Remember, magnificent oak trees begin as little nuts. The creative way is to delay judgment while you are trying to generate new ideas or fresh insights. This opens your self to new possibilities and insights. A research study (New York State University) revealed that about twice as many good ideas are generated when judgment is deferred during the ideation stage of creative problem solving.

When we plant a rose seed, we notice that it is rootless and stemless. Yet we do not criticize it. We treat it as a seed, give it water and fertilize it. When it first shoots up out of the ground, we don't condemn it as scrawny, ugly and underdeveloped with little chance of becoming something of value. As the buds appear, we do not judge their size, shape and form. We understand that it takes time for a seed to become a flower, that within the seed is the potential rose. When the rose finally blooms, we can judge and criticize. Possible we will want to uproot it or poison it and try for a more pleasing variety.

Within each idea there may be a rose; give it a chance--build on it--modify it and strengthen it before you judge it. Poisoning remarks can easily kill an idea before fertile, constructive comments are able to strengthen it and reveal its true potential.

Imagination and judgment are to the thinker what a wrench and screwdriver are to the mechanic. They are two different tools which are used for specific and important purposes. We often use judgment and criticize; however, we are less likely to exercise our imagination, build on ideas and strengthen them. To become creative, we must try to consciously delay our judgment to give our imagination a chance. One hundred and eighty years ago, poet-dramatist Friedrich von Schiller observed, "It hinders the creative work of the mind if the intellect examines too closely the ideas as they pour in." If we are to be creative, we can't step on the brakes and apply the gas at the same time or apply fertilizer simultaneously with poison (see illustration 13). Don't block yourself from an idea or commit yourself to any idea until you've examined as many possible ideas as you can develop.

Don't try to be fertile with ideas and
poison them with judgment at the same time!

Death of An Idea Seed
Illustration 13

Delay judgment on your own ideas as well as those of others. Be open to new experiences and possibilities. Delaying judgment allows our unconscious time to help us get the best answer possible. Delaying judgment for a few minutes helps to separate the use of our creative and judicial tools. Delaying judgment for a long period of time—an hour, day, year—helps keep our conscious mind open to unconscious idea.

Summary

The methods presented herein may or may not work for you. You won't know until you try them. The industrial methods mentioned such as "elimination approach" are designed to meet industries' particular needs. As you work with and study deliberate creative techniques, select and use those which meet your particular needs.

The essence of the processes presented are based on common sense and are not a surprise to anyone. They stress quantity to get quality and delaying judgment. Deliberate creative thinking techniques may be considered as aids to common sense or natural creative thinking. The act of bringing these common sense, natural techniques to consciousness and applying them deliberately will lead to greater creativity. Eventually, after continued use, they restore the strength and vitality of our natural creativity.

Creativity Grows With Exercise!
Deliberate Creativity

1. What is meant by the terms "deliberate creativity," "creative process," and "creative technique"?

2. Use the Procter and Gamble elimination approach to determine:
   a. what things you can eliminate from your daily schedule without harm.

b. what things could be eliminated from your kitchen without reducing its effectiveness.

c. what things you think could be eliminated in present automobiles.

3. Name ten uses for the following: (Feel free to use brainstorming or synectics to help you.)

a. Toothpick.

b. Paper clip.

c. Pencil.

d. Beer mug.

e. Pair of socks.

4. List the attributes of a cloud. Force at least six ideas that these attributes stimulate in your mind about:

a. Your career.

b. Friendship.

c. Creativity.

d. The design of a mail box.

5. List ten things that might happen if we had to walk everywhere we went.

6. Devise, as completely as you can, a creative process checklist.

Quantity of Ideas

1. List five ideas for uses for the following:

a. Coat hanger.

b. Brick.

c. Hairpin.

2. Beauty contests use the idea of quantity to get quality. Name three other areas where it is common to use quantity to get

quality.

3. What are some of the reasons we resist listing many ideas before we choose a good idea?

4. The Neiman-Marcus department store in Texas has advertised unique gifts for the wealthy such as a dinosaur safari, 2,000 year old mummy cases, matching camels, hovercrafts and matching hovercrafts. List 25 ideas for additional gifts for the rich which they might advertise.

5. Develop a list of fifteen possible solutions to the following problems:

   a. How can motorists be encouraged to drive safely?

   b. In what ways can more people be encouraged to vote?

   c. What would be the title for this book?

6. Ask three people for their reaction to the idea that, as Linus Pauling wrote, "The best way to have a good idea is to have lots of ideas." Discuss their comments.

Delaying Judgment

1. Practice in alternating <u>creative thinking and judicial thinking</u>. Write down a problem. Spend 15 minutes and try to come up with good ideas. During the first three minutes, list any <u>good</u> ideas that come to your mind. During the next three minutes, list <u>any</u> ideas (including silly or stupid ideas) that you can think of. Then spend three more minutes thinking judicially, then three minutes thinking creatively and finally three minutes thinking judicially. Discuss how the delaying of judgment during the creative thinking periods affected your results.

2. Delaying judgment in human relations is often beneficial. Ask anyone for some ideas on home decorating. Don't judge the ideas immediately. See if you can build on them--that's transforming them into ideas of value to you before you judge the ideas. Discuss the results.

3. Think of something visual that you never have liked, such as the way someone dresses, neighbor's landscaping, food at a certain restaurant, or another person's style of dress. Look at the object again--now delay judgment and search for its merits for about one minute. Discuss any changes in your view toward the object (if any) that may have resulted from this delaying judgment.

4. The idea of counting to 10 before you speak when you are mad contains an element of delaying judgment. If someone says or has said something which annoys you, delay judgment, ask what they mean and see if this delaying of judgment and clarification of meaning alters your reaction.

5. Discuss the following statement:
Most people prefer to judge ideas, rather than generate them.

Chapter 6

RECOGNIZING CHALLENGES, OPPORTUNITIES AND PROBLEMS
(What if you don't think you have any problems!)

It is difficult to kill a frog by dropping him into hot water. He reacts so quickly to the sudden heat that he jumps out unharmed. But if he is put in cold water and it is warmed up gradually, he doesn't jump out until it is too late. By then he is cooked! Many of the most challenging and important problems in our own lives sneak up on us gradually as with the diver in illustration 14. Before we can solve them, we must first recognize that they are there.

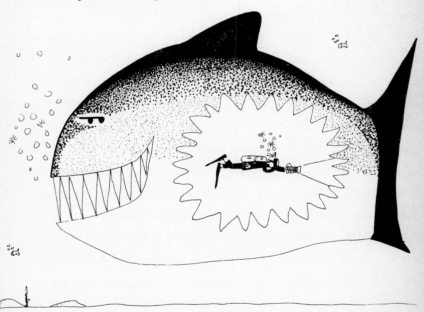

Recognizing Problems
Illustration 14

Solving problems is difficult. Recognizing them is often even more difficult. "The mere formulation of a problem is far more often essential than its solution, which may be merely a matter of mathematical or experimental skill. To raise new questions, new possibilities, to regard old problems from a new angle requires creative imagination and marks real advances in science," wrote Albert Einstein.

George Polya observed that, "Nothing is more interesting for humans than human behavior--and the most characteristically human behavior is solving problems, thinking for a purpose, devising means to some desired end." A problem results from a difference between what exists and what you want to exist. For instance, if you are at home and want to get to work, if the world is hungry and you want to help feed it, if you spill coffee and want it cleaned up, if your child doesn't obey you and you want him to, if you are poor and want to be wealthy, or if cars are unsafe and you want to make them safe. Every personal and professional problem offers a creative challenge. Even the right word at the right time is a creative act.

As creative people, we should place our minds on the pulse of our environment and recognize problems. Problems arise from needs, aggravation, goals, opportunities, voids, trouble shooting, trouble prevention, improving whatever exists and looking into the future.

A leading business consultant remarked that recognizing opportunities, rather than solving problems, was the sign of a top executive. The difficulty in recognizing problems and opportunities is easily observed. For example, one study found that engineering trainees are able to propose very good solutions to problems which are presented to them. However, when they are asked to submit a new problem which would be of value to solve, they encounter great difficulty.

In writing or speech courses, students often do well when responding to assigned topics, but experience difficulty when assigned to develop a topic of their own choice. My experience in creative problem-solving sessions involving participants from many different walks of life, many different ages and levels of intelligence, is that even though they are amazingly good at offering solutions to problems, they usually experience great difficulty when asked to submit a problem to be solved. If I want a moment of dead silence in an otherwise lively creative problem-solving session, I simply need to ask the participants for a problem which we can as a group solve.

William James commented that "part of what we perceive comes through our senses from the object before us; another part (and it may be the larger part) always comes out of our own mind." When we "look" at our lives and environment, our mind places many restraints on what we see depending on our past experiences, attitudes, interests and strengths. To be effective at recognizing (seeing) problems, we must first recognize that we aren't recognizing most of the multitude of problems which surround us.

Recognizing problems on the job, in school, or in society is difficult. However, recognizing problems that we have as an individual is often more difficult and challenging. The central role of psychotherapy and counseling is to help us recognize and face our own problems. This book does not pretend to provide abilities to recognize personal emotional problems. However, as we become more capable of facing and dealing with the problems around us, we also become more capable of facing and dealing with our own personal problems.

A frequent blind spot to problem recognition is problems we once solved which need to be solved again. Mark Twain observed that sometimes we are like a donkey which once it has been burnt by sitting on a hot stone will never sit on a stone again, even when it is cold. We may have early in life solved the problem of how to relate to people. However, if we apply the childhood solution (as some of us do) to adult interactions, we have failed to recognize an obvious problem. If we have designed large cars to meet the desires of the American people, we have solved a problem. However, if as gasoline becomes more and more scarce we haven't introduced compact cars, we have even a bigger problem. We live in an ever-changing society. Problems which not only offer us new challenges and opportunities, but also change the answers to previously solved problems, abound.

Most problem-solving patterns include an evaluation phase. After you have implemented an idea, you should evaluate how well it is "working." The problem-solving pattern presented in Part II of this book does not include such a phase. Rather, evaluation is considered to be an integral, ongoing part of a person's existence. Problems which arise from outside sources, as well as those which arise from ideas which we have tried but aren't performing well, are important to recognize.

The term problem often stimulates negative reactions. Problems are things which many people feel should be avoided rather than face. However, problems also present opportunities for growth and profit and can help us better attain our goals.

Look at what is and then see what could be. A past president of General Motors Corp. credited his company's success to the point of view

that anything and everything--product, process method or human rela-
tions--can be improved. Opportunities sometimes stare you in the face
without being recognized. Frank Epperson recognized an opportunity in
an incident which most of us might have missed.

In 1905, Frank Epperson mixed some soda water powder in a container and left it on the back porch overnight with a spoon accidentally
still in it. The soda pop froze when the nighttime temperatures dropped
to a record low. That was the first popsicle. Epperson later got a patent on the
popsicle. Today Popsicle Industries is a multimillion-dollar business.
Epperson looked beyond the novelty and saw an opportunity for a business.

I wish I could remember what I was planning to do with my life.
You can't get there if you don't know where you are going. An old
proverb states, "He travels furthest who knows his destination." A
child soon learns to walk but may never know where he is going. Very
few of us very seriously and systematically examine our personal and
professional goals. And, even if we do, we don't recognize them as
challenging problems which can be creatively solved. Goals help us
focus on our destination or objectives in many areas, such as career,
personal relationships, physical condition, recreation and education.

Family, spiritual and individual growth, health, skill and career
improvement all offer creative challenges. An important part of goal
achievement is the careful selection and clear statement of the goal.
Because once you state a goal, it has a way of becoming self-fulfilling.
We are spurred on by goals. And, as we discussed earlier, the unconscious mind's problem-solving ability is engaged to help us achieve it.

As with the scuba diver in illustration 15, some problems are easy to recognize. However, more often they are not. Recognizing problems is a creative art and skill which can be developed. It is developed by understanding and practice which lead to the self-confidence necessary to face them.

We are often despondent when we observe too many problems. However, be thankful for problems. They not only stretch our imagination and provide us food for thought, they provide most people with their livelihood. If people didn't make mistakes, things didn't go wrong, and if difficult problems did not exist, much of our work would not be needed and we might be out of work. If we recognize more problems and learn how to solve them creatively as opportunities rather than irritations, we will enjoy a more happy, productive and successful life.

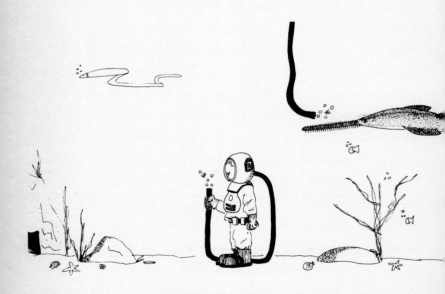

The Obvious Problem
Illustration 15

The most rewarding goals and challenging problems and opportunities are not the same for each of us. A meaningful challenge to one person may prove to be a bore to another. An artist and scientist will not likely be challenged by the same professional problem. This book cannot provide each of you with problems which challenge you to think your creative best. However, if you do the exercises in this chapter and save the results, you will have problems, goals and challenges which are of value to you and will enhance you when you try to solve them.

The Ability to Recognize Problems Grows with Exercise!

Note: a. When a problem is written, begin it with "In what ways..." instead of "How..." or some other prefix. This approach opens the way to a variety of solutions instead of only one.

b. In these exercises we are searching for problems not solutions. State problems which the exercises stimulate. Don't worry about being able to solve them!

1. Discuss the following quotations:

a. "If a man looks sharply and attentively, he shall see Fortune; for, though she is blind, she is not invisible."

Francis Bacon

b. "They say a reasonable number of fleas is good fer a dog - keeps him from broodin' over bein' a dog." Edward Westcott

2. Imagine possible dissatisfactions with the following items and state several problems which may result.

a. living room furniture

For example, I am dissatisfied with the height of the seat on most chairs. Problem - In what ways can the seat height of chairs be altered to meet the needs of tall people?

    b.   the gasoline automobile

    c.   your personal relationships at home

    d.   your personal relationships on the job

    e.   your personal relationships at school

    f.   your daily routine

    g.   world peace

3. Recognize opportunities or benefits in the following problems.

    For example: The Problem - "I need a job to finance education" presents the opportunity to gain work experience, meet other people on the job and become more familiar with personal finances.

    a.   I need to get up at 6 a.m. to go to work.

    b.   I must cut the lawn once a week.

    c.   I have not achieved much material success in life.

4. Ask three people to mention aggravations (annoyances) which they face. Write down problem statements which these aggravations suggest.

5. List ten possible barriers to people recognizing problems.

6. List at least five annoyances (aggravations) which you encounter during the next twenty-four hours. Write down problems that these annoyances might suggest. For example, it is hard for me to wake up in the morning. Problem: In what ways can I make it easier for me to wake up in the morning?

7. Envision your desired work situation, hobbies, vacations, family and home to be twenty years from now. List five challenges which you face between now and twenty years from now if you are to achieve your vision.

8. List five challenges which a dog faces in life. List at least three problems which we face which are similar to those you listed for a dog. For example, a dog faces the problem of getting enough attention (strokes) - so do we.

9. List a minimum of five problems suggested by your pet peeves, things which bore you, things you put off, things you like or don't like in others, how you want others to think of you, and things which excite you.

10. List a minimum of five problems which people encounter in each of the following areas:

    a. in a classroom.

    b. at home.

    c. at work.

    d. in politics.

    e. in achieving wealth.

    f. in achieving health.

    g. in making friends.

    h. in keeping peace in the world.

11. Perform a quick lifetime goals analysis.

    a. In two minutes write down, <u>as fast as you can</u>, your lifetime goals relating to personal, family, social, career, financial and spiritual areas. (List 1).

    b. Spend another minute or two clearing up, clarifying and adding to those goals.

    c. In two minutes write down, <u>as fast as you can</u>, how you would like to spend the next two years of your life. (List 2). Be creative. List even those fantasy goals you may desire, such as to become famous.

d. Spend another minute or two clearing up, clarifying and adding to these goals.

e. In two minutes write down what you would do during the next three months, if you knew you were going to die in three months. (List 3).

f. Review all three lists of goals for a few minutes, adding to and clarifying them.

g. From these nine goals, select the one from each list that you feel is most important to begin working on immediately. These three goals provide problems which you may wish to use your creativity to solve.

12. Read one newspaper. List ten problems in society which it suggests.

13. Using any or all of the previous exercises, develop a list of at least fifty goals, opportunities or problems which you would like to solve.

P A R T   I I

A CREATIVE PROCESS AND CREATIVE CATALYSTS

In the area of human behavior we frequently try to defy nature's gravity by designing waterways which flow uphill. The process and patterns for creative thinking which we advocate defy human nature. The process and catalysts presented in this book are designed to strengthen and amplify our natural creative thinking process and overcome poor thinking habits which tend to restrict our creativity.

This process and the catalysts are a synthesis of the catalysts such as brainstorming and synectics, which already exist and ones which I have formulated based on my educational, research and professional experience in engineering, psychology, education, leadership and administration. They are workable, usable processes which have been tested on thousands of people and can be readily integrated into everyday and professional thinking patterns. They can be used to aid the solution of small problems; for example, what should I buy someone for someone's birthday, as well as large ones, such as in what ways can a cheap source of power be developed for the world.

They can be used in a "sit down," "here and now" problem-solving
situation or combined with research and incubation for long-term problem-
solving efforts. The emphasis in this book is on the "sit down," "here
and now" problems where little time is available for research and incubation. We engage in this type of problem solving most frequently.

These processes and catalysts can be used by groups of people or
by individuals. We solve most problems while working alone. Therefore,
this mode of problem solving is stressed. Frequently a combination of
individual and group problem solving achieves the most effective results.

The process presented in this part of the text is designed to help
you organize your problem solving into four phases: define the problem,
open yourself to many possible solutions, identify and intensify the best
solution and transform the solution into action. The first letters of
the Define, Open, Identify, and Transform steps or phases form the acronym DO IT which is the name of the process. The acronym has much greater
meaning than simply Define, Open, Identify and Transformation. It is a
call for action. Do it. Use the process and the catalyst to help you
become more creative. DO IT creatively and often.

The steps in the DO IT process are simple and straightforward.
Define the problem to make sure you are solving the real problem and to
help engage your conscious and unconscious mind to the problem. Open
yourself to consider many diverse solution ideas. Delay judgment on
the ideas generated until the Identify step. Then Identify the best
solution to your problem and modify it until you are ready to transform
your idea into action. Transform your solution idea into action.

The DO IT process is similar to good systematic industrial and personal problem solving efforts. It offers a systems approach similar to

that used in industry combined with catalysts for creative thinking which are intertwined in the fabric of the DO IT process. The catalyst are designed to accelerate our creative thinking.

Even when we have a good plan or process, it isn't always easy to follow because we are usually too eager to sacrifice quality and originality for the security offered by an immediate solution to our problems. The DO IT catalyst stimulates creative solutions throughout the problem-solving process and at the same time provides periods of rest, fun and excitement within the sometimes slow and dull but necessary process.

Most catalysts or stimulators of creative thought such as brainstorming place overwhelming emphasis on the Open phase of problem solving. They focus on the generation of ideas. The DO IT catalysts, in addition to helping us generate creative ideas, provide tools for the creative definition of the problem, modification and strengthening of the solution idea and motivation to get off the spot and transform our ideas into action.

Most people need the greatest help in generating large numbers of good, original ideas; however, some people easily generate lots of ideas but the ideas fall around them like leaves off a tree and rot. They aren't able to polish them and transform them into action. Others are able to obtain many great ideas to the wrong problem. They define the problem so poorly that their creative ideas are of no value to their real original purpose. The DO IT process and catalysts offer help and stimulation for each of these people. It can be used in part or as a whole, depending on the unique person and problems involved.

The DO IT catalysts which help to solve problems at the definition stage are Mind Focus, Mind Grip and Mind Stretch. The catalysts which emphasize the production of large numbers of original ideas are Mind Prompt, Mind Surprise, Mind Free and Mind Synthesize. The catalysts which emphasize the solution identification and simplification of ideas are Mind Integrate and Mind Strengthen. The Mind Energize catalyst helps you to decide to either make the commitment required to transform the idea into a reality or to forget the solution and move on to a new problem. Table one lists the catalysts and a brief statement about their use.

Part II of this text is devoted to exploring and developing skill in the use of these catalysts. In golf and tennis one of the fundamental rules is to "keep your eye on the ball." Those who have tried to apply this "simple" rule understand that it takes practice to achieve. They also know how important it is to playing the sport well. Similarly, these creativity catalysts are not complicated. However, they can only become effective tools through practice. They are the fundamentally important tools for creative problem solving.

The DO IT Creatively Catalysts

Catalysts for defining the problem

Mind Focus
1. Ask why the problem exists. This may lead to a broader statement of the problem.
2. Try to subdivide the problem into smaller problems. This may lead to a narrower restatement of the problem.

Mind Grip
Write down at least three two-word statements of the problem's objective. Select the combination of words which best represents the precise problem you want to solve. Use this to write a new, more optimal and effective restatement of the problem.

Mind Stretch
List the goals, objectives and/or criteria which you want the solution of the problem to satisfy. (Think of obstacles which must be overcome.) Then stretch each goal, objective or criterion and write down any ideas which are stimulated.

Catalysts for developing many diverse ideas

Mind Prompt
Ask other people with diverse backgrounds, knowledge and intelligence for solutions to your problem. Use their ideas as prompters for your own ideas.

Mind Surprise
List ridiculous, laughable ideas. Use them to trigger more reasonable, possibly usable solutions to your problem.

Mind Free
Stimulate fresh ideas by forcing similarities between your problem and things which aren't logically related to your problem.

Table 1

1. Write down the name of a physical object, picture, plant or animal.
2. List its characteristics in detail.
3. Use the listed characteristics to stimulate insights into the ideas for the solution of your problem.

Mind Synthesize   Use logical combinations of ideas already collected to stimulate new ideas.

Catalysts for identifying the best idea

Mind Integrate   Review your goals, objectives and/or criteria, then trust your own gut-level feeling to select the best idea.

Mind Strengthen   List the negative aspects of your idea. Be vicious! Try to positivize the negatives. Then modify the solution to reduce the negative aspects.

Mind Energize   Exaggerate the worst and best potential consequence which might result from implementation of your solution. Modify your solution to minimize bad consequences and maximize good consequences.

Table 1 (Cont.)

The central strategy and strength of doing it creatively is to integrate immediate results and long-term preparations, systematic serious
thinking and relaxed and fun type thinking, adult type thinking and
childlike imagination, structure and freedom, and judgment and criticism. The DO IT process provides the structure and the DO IT catalysts
stimulate the creativity within the structure. They offer keys to our
locked up creative potential (see illustration 16).

Keys to Creative Problem Solving
Illustration 16

Sometimes the DO IT process and catalysts are regarded as scien-
tific formulas. However, they are not strict, unswerving formulas;
rather they are flexible, adaptable aids to the effective use of your
natural problem-solving process. The DO IT process and catalysts are

tools for thinking. They can be compared to the tools used by a skillful mechanic. The mechanic uses them according to the specific need at the time. The DO IT process and catalysts are presented to enlarge the reader's choice of mental tools.

The benefits of creative thinking outlined earlier in the section entitled "Why Do People Create?" are enormous. Skill in creative thinking is vitally important and is available to virtually everyone. As with other areas in human behavior, no one can prove this to you. Only you can. As Galileo wrote, "You cannot teach a man anything, you can only help him to find it within himself." In this section of the book insights and exercises are provided to help stimulate your learning. The rest is up to you.

Chapter 7

DEFINING THE PROBLEM

If you are able to state a problem, it can be solved. Sounds easy, doesn't it! On the other hand, Einstein remarked that the mere formulation of a problem is far more often essential than the solution, which may be merely a matter of mathematical or experimental skills. A friend of mine, who is a partner in a value engineering firm, told me that about one third of the time in his training workshops for industrial design engineers is spent developing the skill of properly defining a problem. Proper problem definition is very important. As an old proverb states, "Well begun is half done."

In spite of the importance of this phase of problem solving, we usually spend only a few seconds, if any, consciously and carefully defining and trying to understand exactly what the problem is that we face. Extra minutes spent giving a clearer definition of the problem may be worth hours, days or even years spent correcting a poor solution to an unclear problem.

Many times we come up with solutions in search of a problem. To most of us, it is easier to come up with solutions than it is to define a problem. We want results and are impatient with the not obviously productive time spent defining the problem.

Some of us live our lives in a manner which is a good solution to the wrong or poorly defined problem. We get rich when what we really wanted was genuine friendship. We get free time for leisure when what we really thrive on is meaningful work. Careful definition of the problem not only helps to insure that we are solving the "right" problem, it provides us with an overview of the problem. This helps provide a specific focus for our problem-solving energy. It also helps us to engage our conscious and unconscious minds to the problem-solving effort.

The definition stage of the problem-solving process is our first major conscious encounter with the problem. If done with sufficient intensity and commitment, this conscious encounter may engage firmly our unconscious mind as a formidable ally to our problem-solving effort. Remember that the unconscious mind is generally considered to be the most powerful aid to natural creative problem solving. If we consider the problem to be important and carefully define it, our unconscious mind may become caught up in, and intensely involved in, an effort to solve the problem we define for it. The unconscious mind follows and is led by conscious interest, concentration and focus.

The definition process can be aided by utilizing the DO IT catalysts; Mind Focus, Mind Grip and Mind Stretch. Mind Focus helps us focus our energies on the exact problem which we wish to solve. Mind Grip helps us economically and optimally determine the essence of the definition of our problem. Mind Stretch helps us think big for a moment, get a firm feel for the boundaries of the problem and develop fresh original solution ideas. Problem definition is also aided by writing problem statements down on paper. As Francis Bacon observed, "Writing maketh the exact man."

Sometimes the results of carefully and accurately defining a problem do not appear to be commensurate with the time spent defining the problem. Only a small change of the original problem statement may occur. However, a small change at the beginning can make a big change

at the end. A small error in aiming a rifle can result in a major miss
of the target. In addition, even if no change occurs in the definition
of the problem, we benefit from the definition effort because our powerful unconscious problem-solving ability is engaged by this activity.

Focus on the Real Problem (Mind Focus)

It's what we do that counts--not how much we do. It's solving the
right problem that counts--not the amount of problem solving. Consider
the scuba diver engulfed by the shark at the beginning of Chapter 6.
Once he recognized that he had a problem, he could state it in several
ways: In what ways can I get out of this shark? How can I survive
while in here? In what ways can I get the shark to let me out? How
can I leave a last will and testament and get it to my relatives? How
can I kill this shark? How can I die gracefully? Usually we immediately
seize on one of these definitions without considering other possible
definitions, and concentrate all of our energies on its solution.

A great solution to the problem of how can I die gracefully in the
shark would be much less valuable than a poor solution to the problem
of how can I get out of this shark? The value of our problem solving
effort is a direct function of how accurately we are able to focus on
the real, most important statement of the problem.

Sometimes we are unable to see the forest because of the trees, or
the trees because of the forest, or a leaf because of the trees. To see
clearly what we want to see requires a proper focus of our concentration. If we don't know exactly what we are looking for, we will probably find something else. If we don't know where we are going, we will
probably end up somewhere else. If we aren't able to focus on the precise problem which is of most value for us to solve, we will probably

end up solving the wrong problem or a less valuable problem. As a result of focusing on the wrong problem, we often create new problems, and one of the unfortunate truths of life is that problems which we create ourselves are the hardest problems to solve.

Our mind's energies are generally diffuse like the sun falling evenly over the surface of the earth. The mind-focusing catalyst called Mind Focus is designed to help us concentrate and focus our energies onto one problem. Then, like the burning focused power of a magnifying glass, our mind's energy can burn a solution to the problem (see illustration 17).

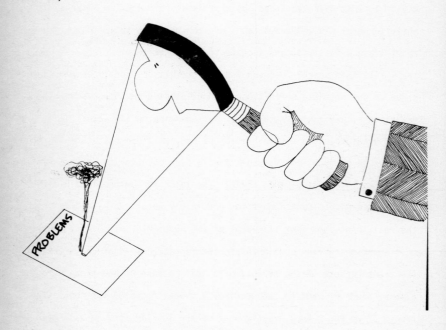

Mind Focus
Illustration 17

Proper focus provides effective use of our energy. Squeeze your fist as tight as possible. Notice the tenseness in your forearm and fist. Now relax your forearm and, at the same time, squeeze your fist as hard as before, if not harder. Relaxing your forearm allows you to focus your strength on your fist. Mind Focus helps provide an optional statement of the problem so that we can refocus our mental powers onto the right problem.

Frequently a proper definition of the problem is so powerful that the answer is more or less obvious, or our unconscious mind is able to make the answer obvious without additional conscious effort. The value of focus is obvious in physically oriented skills. For example, in tennis or golf, the need to focus on the ball is a matter of athletic survival. Once we take our eye's focus off the ball, our level of play drops drastically.

When Arturo Toscanini was 80, his son asked the conductor what he considered his most important achievement. The answer was: "Whatever he happens to be doing at the moment, is the biggest thing in his life, whether he is conducting a symphony or peeling an orange."

Toscanini's success and that of athletes, businessmen, artists, writers and scientists depends to a great extent on their ability to optimally focus their energies. Our ability to focus our energies on the right problem is also a prime determinant in our success as problem solvers.

Optimal focus is only achieved after many focusing tries. Over-focus can be just as damaging as under-focus. We have a limited amount of mental energy which must be allocated carefully.

If we are driving down a freeway with our conscious mind focused on a non-driving problem, we may lose our life in an accident. Some people focus so much energy on part of the problem that they totally ignore other important aspects of it. The commitment to one goal or problem necessarily involves the sacrifice or slighting of other problems.

One of my college students used Maxwell Maltz's approach to focusing (discussed in Chapter 5) to focus her energies on her desire to be promoted to a higher position in her company. It worked. She got the promotion. However, she complained that she would not do it again because too much of her energy was focused on that single goal. Other important aspects of her life were neglected, such as good social relations and physical fitness.

A man I know ate lunch with psychologist Fritz Perls, the father of Gestalt therapy. Perls did not speak to him during the entire lunch and rarely even looked up from his meal. Perls placed such great emphasis on the importance of focusing on the "here and now." His "here and now" was his meal on which he focused his total energies to the exclusion of his luncheon companion. Focusing requires a choice between doing a a few things well and doing many poorly. The professor in illustration 18 was obviously focusing too much of his thought on his teaching and not enough on his personal appearance.

Over Focus
Illustration 18

The Mind Focusing catalyst is twofold. We ask ourselves why the problem exists. This may lead to a broader focus on the problem and to a greater number and variety of solutions. We then try to subdivide the statement of the problem to determine if it would be better to focus our energy on a more specific aspect of the problem.

Ask Why

Frequently, problem statements are so specific or narrow that many possibly good solutions are eliminated from consideration. A student with a cart loaded with experimental equipment poised at the bottom of a flight of stairs asked a passerby for help. He was trying to decide how to get the cart and equipment up the stairs. He had considered finding several people to help him carry it up as one piece; or, carrying the cart and equipment up separately. When he was asked what his problem was, he responded that it was to get the cart and equipment up the stairs. The passerby's suggestion was to use the elevator, which he was aware of and which was located a short distance from the stairs.

This particular student is very bright and alert. Yet, because he defined his problem too narrowly, "How to get the equipment up the stairs," instead of more broadly, "How can I get the equipment from the second to the third floor?," he was locked into poor solutions. The use of the elevator seems obvious, and that a bright person would not use it seems ridiculous. Problems are often caused by a poor definition of the problem.

Asking "why" the problem exists may lead to a broader problem statement which is more appropriate to the problem we face. Why did the student want to get the equipment to the top of the stairs? To get the equipment to the third floor. So a better problem statement would have been, "In what ways can the equipment be moved from the second to the third floor?"

An engineering supervisor observed a persistent traffic jam at a particular point on a freeway. What follows are possible definitions of this problem and associated possible solutions. "Why" is used to obtain broader problem statements.

Problem Statements	Possible Solutions
Initial Problem Statement.	
In what ways can the freeway be widened to increase traffic flow? <u>Why</u> widen the freeway?	Increase the width by adding another l
Answer: To increase traffic flow!	
First Restatement of the Problem.	Widen the freeway. Double deck
In what ways can the flow of traffic be increased?	freeway. Increased speed limit. Use narrower lanes. Use existing freeway shoulder as a lane

-108-

Problem Statements	Possible Solutions
	or as part of a lane.

Why increase traffic flow?
Answer: To increase the flow of
people past a particular point on
the freeway.

Second Restatement of the Problem.	
In what ways can the flow of	All of the solutions to the
people past this point on the	first two problem statements.
freeway be increased?	Also, require car pools and in-
	creased train and bus service.

Why increase the flow of
people?
Answer: To alleviate traffic con-
gestion.

Third Restatement of the Problem.	
In what ways can we alleviate	All of the solutions to the three
traffic congestion at this	problem statements. Also, adver-
point on the freeway?	tise the congestion problem and
	suggest alternate routes. Stag-
	ger starting and ending work
	times at large local industries.
	Close On ramps near this point
	on the freeway during peak peri-
	ods of congestion.

The initial problem statement contained its own solution: Widen
the freeway. MIT professor, A. H. Keil, observed that most frequently
the initial statement of a need to the engineering community is also a
preconceived solution.

Each "why" question in this example led to a broader statement of
the problem and eliminated dependence on preconceived solutions. Possible solutions to the broader statement include all solutions for the
more narrow statements. Therefore, the positive advantage of asking

"why" is that it opens the way to more, and possibly better, alternative solutions to the problem. The negative aspect of broadening a definition is that the problem statement may become so broad that it is difficult to readily focus on. Then our mental energy is wasted on many useless solutions. What we need is an optimal statement of the problem—not too broad, yet not too narrow.

Observe the increase in amount and diversity of potential solutions, which results from asking "why the problem exists," for the problem: "Invent a better mouse trap."

Problem Statements	Possible Solutions
Initial Problem Statement.	
Invent a better mouse trap.	Modification of the existing
Why invent a better mouse trap?	mouse traps. Bear type trap.
Answer: To kill mice.	
First Restatement of the Problem.	All of the solutions to the ini-
In what ways can we kill mice?	tial problem statement. Also,
Why kill mice?	poison, explosive devices, clamp-
Answer: To get rid of them from	ing devices or a cat.
homes.	
Second Restatement of the Problem.	
In what ways can mice be elimi-	All of the solutions to the first
nated from homes?	two problems. Also, perhaps a
Why eliminate mice from homes?	vibration, noise or smell would
Answer: Because they often enter	drive them out. Clean up mouse-
the home from nearby fields.	attracting debris.
Third Restatement of the Problem.	
In what ways can we keep mice	All of the solutions to the first
from entering our homes?	three problems. Also, place traps
	or poison at the point of mouse
	entry into the house. Keep sever-
	al cats outside the house. Place
	screens over points of entry.

When a problem is broadened by asking "why," the solutions to earlier narrow problem statements remain available. However, in addition to those solutions, more possible solutions are stimulated. We may solve the mouse problem by using poison or we may ultimately choose to modify any existing type of mouse trap (the first solution). However, even in this case, we have only lost a few minutes by considering other possible problem statements and associated solutions, and we have gained confidence that the solution we finally select is the best one.

John E. Arnold, late professor of engineering, put the matter of broadening the statement of a problem this way: "Knowing what you are looking for helps you to recognize it when you see it. But in the case of innovation, how do you know what you are looking for? You don't, unless you state your problem so broadly, so basically, so all-inclusively and generically that you do not preclude even the remotest possibilities—so that you do not pre-condition your mind to a narrow range of acceptable answers."

Consider the problem of deciding how to decorate the interior of a home. Some reasons "why" we might decorate our home include: To make the inside more beautiful, appealing, interesting, impressive, easier to clean or easier to sell. If the "real" reason for decorating is to prepare the home for resale, the problem should be stated as, "In what ways can the inside of our home be decorated to increase the resale value?" This problem statement will lead to better solutions than if the problem is stated as, "How can I decorate my house?" The solution will be more concerned with the decorating tastes of the general public and less concerned with those of the present owner who may soon be moving. This asking "why" led to a narrower, more properly focused problem statement.

If you feel that you want to become wealthy: Possible reasons "why" you might want to become wealthy include: To gain security, power, influence, enjoyment of life, respect of others, self-respect or early retirement. If the primary reason for wanting to become wealthy is to retire early, the real problem you face is, "In what ways can I retire early?" Possible reasons "why" someone might want to retire early include: To stop having to work for someone else, to be able to fish every day or to be able to travel and relax. If the real reason for wanting to retire early is to be able to travel, solutions might include: Becoming a travel agent, joining the Peace Corps, becoming a traveling salesman or joining the diplomatic corps, instead of trying to become wealthy.

All of these solutions may be better for an individual than putting off travel until they are rich. They may never become rich. The restatements of the problem, which the question "why" helped to develop, focused the problem-solving efforts more directly on the real problem and provided more useful solutions.

Subdivide (Divide and Conquer)

If we were asked to design a car, out of necessity we would divide the problem into sub-problems (smaller problems), such as body design, engine design, wheel design and interior design. Furthermore, each of these problems would be subdivided. For example, body design might include style, aerodynamics, ease of entering and exiting, ease of repair, and ease of manufacture. Each of these subdivisions provides a better focus for our designing talents and energy.

This book is subdivided into chapters and subheadings to provide focus on certain aspects of creative problem solving and to make it easier to write, comprehend, use and refer to. Military people try to divide their enemy into smaller parts, then focus the majority of their energies on conquering the small part as a way to win the larger war. As an old proverb says, "A thousand-mile journey begins with the first step."

Osborn, the father of brainstorming, observed that problem statements for group brainstorming should be specific rather than general. They should be "narrowed down so that the panel members can shoot their ideas at a single target." Subdivison is one approach to narrowing the problem.

The freeway problem, "In what ways can the freeway be widened," could be subdivided into sub-problems with focus on the amount of widening needed, the type of freeway surfaces to be used and the method of installation. The problem of decorating a home could be subdivided into decorating problems for the various rooms, use of wallpaper, use of mirrors or paint, type of furniture, furniture arrangement and ease of maintenance. The design of a mouse trap could be subdivided into the trap mechanism design, materials to be used, how to set the trap, how to dispose of the mouse, the bait to use and the aesthetics of the design.

All problems can be subdivided. They can be subdivided by function (purpose); for example, setting the trap versus releasing the mouse, by components; decoration of the bedroom versus the living room, and by timing; for example, what deadlines need to be met for the initial and final design.

Improving new designs or modifying existing designs can be greatly helped by the process of subdivision. For example, this book could be subdivided by function into pages, method of holding pages together, and cover. Focusing on the subproblem of holding the pages together: glue, spiral, clamps, steel rings or staples might be used. Focusing on the subproblem of type of paper: type of plastic, cardboard, newsprint or art paper might be used. Focusing on the subproblem of the book's cover: no cover, cardboard, paper, metal or plastic covers might be considered. Many possible books might be designed utilizing various combinations of the ideas generated for each of these subproblems. We could design a cheap text with no cover, stapled together and using newsprint paper, or we might choose a more substantial one with a metal cover, plastic pages and bound with steel rings.

The inventor, Charles F. Kettering, wrote, "The process of research is to pull the problem apart into its different elements, a great many of which you already know about. Then you can work on the things you don't know about." Subdividing a problem helps us to focus on the most important aspect of the problem.

Summary of Mind Focus

When everything is important, nothing is important. If we develop too many goals and subproblems which we wish to solve, it may become impossible to solve any of them (see illustration 19). I have enjoyed the sports of basketball, tennis, volleyball and badminton. I am interested in engineering, science, psychology, music and art. I have devoted some of my energies to, and tried to succeed in, each of these areas. It took the first thirty-five years of my life to fully realize that nobody can do everything, an apparently obvious thought. When I finally truly accepted that fact, focused on one or two areas, I became much more relaxed, effective and successful. I still have a variety of interests and activities; however, I don't try to excel in all of them.

Lack of Focus
Illustration 19

Business, college and industrial executives are usually faced with many problems. If they tried to solve all of them, they would solve few of them well. Like the carpenter who tries to hammer more than one nail at a time, their efforts would lead to bent nails. When operating effectively, we should recognize and list all of our problems, then arrange and solve them according to their order of importance. If some of the less important problems aren't solved, that is a sacrifice we must make in order to solve the most important ones.

We need to keep our eye on the overall problem but solve each of the subproblems as they come. Tennis players must continuously keep their eye on the ball and control it to solve their overall problem of winning the game. However, many subproblems must be focused on and solved along the way. Where and how hard should I hit the serve, volley or ground stroke? Where should I position myself on the court and when should I rush the net?

Which subproblem we begin with depends on which one we feel is the most important. As with becoming a better tennis player, we could work on our serving, backhand or ground stroke. The use of our "gut-level feeling," combined with conscious deliberation, is the best way to make the choice as to which problem to solve first.

Creativity Grows with Exercise! (Mind Focus)

1. List a minimum of three possible reasons "why" the following problems exist and then three restatements of the problem which the resultant reason suggests. (Don't worry about obtaining a solution now.)

    a. What should I wear for Church on Sunday?

    b. In what ways can the design of a kitchen table be improved?

    c. In what ways can I help achieve world peace?

2. List at least three attributes (characteristics) of each of the following: (Attributes of a problem lead to subproblems.)

    a. Education.

    b. Light bulb.

    c. Vacation at the beach.

    d. Getting a job.

    e. Chair.

    f. Speech.

3. List at least three subproblems which the problems in question 2 suggest.

4. Discuss the following statements:

    a. "To do two things at once is to do neither." Publilius Syrus

    b. You will never get there if you don't know where you are going.

5. List at least three different, more general or more specific, ways
   of stating the following problems:

   a. In what ways can I achieve greater happiness?

   b. In what ways can the design of a bathroom be improved?

   c. In what ways can airplanes be made safer?

   d. In what ways can I spend my free time?

   e. In what ways can I be more creative?

   f. In what ways can the design of a pencil be improved?

6. In what ways can you mix efforts to accomplish (focus on) current
   demands as well as plan and prepare for future activity?

7. Apply Mind Focus to a problem of your own.

Get a Firm Grip on the Problem (Mind Grip)

Muhammad Ali, the world champion heavyweight boxer, observed that
he usually softens up his opponent and feels him out with light punches
before he is ready to release his "big punch." He in effect defined
the problem with his light punches before he solved it. Golfers know
the importance of getting a firm, precise grip on their golf club. If
the club is rotated in the hand or finger or thumb slightly out of position, the ball will fly way off course (see illustration 20).

The catalyst Mind Grip is designed to help us get a firm, precise
hold on often slippery, vague and poorly defined problems. It leads to
a more economical, optimal statement of the problem. The amount of
change in the problem may be small, but the change in the value of the
solution, due to this small change in the problem definition, can be
enormous. In addition, Mind Grip helps to engage the conscious and unconscious mind to the problem more effectively.

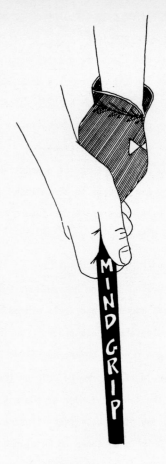

Mind Grip
Illustration 20

"The obvious is always least understood," according to Prince
Metternich. Mind gripping may be considered a way of making sure we
understand obvious problem statements. Mind gripping helps us develop a
clear, brief and simple statement of the problem. As Albert Einstein

observed, "Everything should be made as simple as possible, but not simpler." To be able to write such a statement, we need to clear our mind of trivialities, wrong emphasis and incorrect information. As one college president remarked, creative people can look at relatively complex situations and bring into them a simple focus.

The essence of Mind Grip is to transform primitive, flabby, wordy and hazy problem statements into a two-word, simple statement of the problem which captures the central objective of the problem. It is based on the business axiom of simplicity KISS -- Keep It Simple Stupid. Consider the problem of developing a better paper clip holder. Our objective is to design a paper clip holder. We might define our objective more specifically: to design a paper clip container, dispenser or paper clip storage. If we ultimately decide to design a paper clip dispenser, instead of a paper clip holder as originally stated, we have made a small change in the problem statement but a big change in the types of possible solutions. We would concentrate our energies on designs for a dispenser of paper clips, instead of designs for a holder.

Once the two-word statement of the objective of the problem is identified, two columns of words which might be used in place of the originally used words are written down. From the two lists, the combinations of words which best represent the problem are selected. The problem is then restated using these two words to provide a better grip on the exact nature of the problem.

For example, in what ways can I get to sleep easier at night? Sleep easier is the initial two-word objective of the problem. A list of similar words follows:

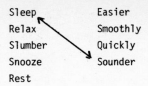

Sleep	Easier
Relax	Smoothly
Slumber	Quickly
Snooze	Sounder
Rest	

A thesaurus is helpful for developing the lists of alternate but similar words. Using the words "sleep sounder," I would restate this problem as, "In what ways can I sleep sounder at night?" To sleep easier tends to focus on ways of getting to sleep, whereas to sleep sounder tends to emphasize obtaining the most from the reenergizing effects of sleep, which is what I would be most interested in. You may feel some other word combination would lead to a better statement of the problem, depending on your needs and desires.

Consider the problem, "In what ways can the productivity of the automobile production line workers be increased?" "Increased productivity" is the two-word objective of the problem. Lists of similar words follow.

Increase	Productivity
Improve	Work load
Enlarge	Work output
Accelerate	Efficiency
Augment	Effectiveness
Double	Energy
	Fruitful

My choice was to use "improve efficiency," as the best specific two-word problem objective statement. The restated problem is then, "In what ways can the efficiency of automobile production line workers be increased?" The choice of words depends on the actual facts surrounding the problem and your personal experience, which interprets these facts. Even though many possible combinations exist, when a group of knowledgeable people in a company make such a selection, the majority usually choose the same combination of words.

The mind grip catalyst is not very complicated or time consuming and it may change the problem statement only slightly. However, it may have a dramatic effect on the value of the solution to the problem. Like a small change in the grip of a golfer, course of a missile, or tuning of a piano, it may have a dramatic effect on the results.

Creativity Grows with Exercise! (Mind Grip)

1. Develop five two-word statements of the objective to the following problems. Select the combination which you feel is best and write a restatement of each problem.

   a. Think of ten ways a child of five could amuse herself on a long car trip.

   b. In what ways can marriage ceremonies be improved?

   c. Invent a better garbage can.

   d. In what ways can we insure that we eat better?

2. By mind gripping, you are in effect striving for a better name for a problem's objective. List three different names for the following items. Circle the one which you feel best fits the item. For example, a spoon might be called a scoop, shovel or feeder.

   a. Chair.

   b. Pencil.

   c. Hat.

   d. President.

   e. Mountain.

   f. Duck.

3. Develop five new names for a book on highway safety. Circle the one you like best.

4. For the Olympics, you are invited to invent a new word for common items to promote international communication. Try to invent new words for the following items:

   a. Basketball.

   b. High jump.

   c. Tumbling.

   d. Bathroom.

   e. Shot put.

   f. Boxing.

5. Write the words in exercise two vertically. Write a word beginning with each letter of the word which relates to the total word. For example, using the word Chair we could obtain:

   C omfortable

   H elpful

   A rtful

   I dentifiable

   R elaxing

6. Select three problems you wish to solve. Use Mind Grip to develop the most optimal, simple statement to each of these three problems.

Think Big (Mind Stretch)

Charles Kettering observed that a person with a hazy goal never exceeds a hazy goal. If a circle is drawn around our target, it is easier to hit. Criteria, short-term and long-term goals and objectives for what we hope to get from the solution to a problem, help define the boundaries of our possible problem solutions. We may want the mouse trap design to be cheap, attractive, simple, long-lasting and easy to use. These objectives and goals for our design help us focus on good solutions by

excluding very expensive, unattractive, complex, short-lived or diffi-
cult-to-use design possibilities. These goals and objectives also
provide us criteria or "yardsticks" against which we can evaluate alternative designs to select the best one.

On the other hand, these same aids to problem solving goals, objectives and criteria may hinder the production of fresh, new, creative
ideas. They may cause us to prematurely reject any ideas which at
first glance do not appear to meet our initial goals, objectives and
criteria, but which could be modified later to meet them.

Try to draw four continuous straight lines, connected at the ends,
which will pass through the nine dots below. The lines can intersect,
but cannot be retraced.

```
        .        .        .


        .        .        .


        .        .        .
```

Be creative - try many possibilities. Try drawing lines which
penetrate the boundaries of the dots. Turn to the exercises at the
end of this chapter to see the solution. This is a difficult problem
to solve with or without hints. One of the major difficulties in solving it arises from our own self-imposed, or perhaps we should say habit-
imposed boundaries to the problem. A common mistake of engineers, businessmen and most people is to never think big enough. We like to be
sure of what we are doing and stay within often artificial boundaries.
The resistance to drawing lines which penetrated the apparent boundaries
of the dots is an unrealistic habitual restraint.

Kafka wrote, "Every man lives behind bars, which he carries with him. That is why people write so much about animals. It's an expression of longing for a free natural life. But for human beings the natural life is a human life, but we don't always realize that. They refuse to realize it. Human existence is a burden to them, so they dispose of their fantasies. Safe in the shelter of the herd, they march through the streets of the cities to their way to work, to their feeding troughs, to their pleasures. There are no longer marvels; only regulations, prescriptions, directives. Men are afraid of freedom and responsibility. They prefer to hide behind the prison bars which they build around themselves."

The Mind Stretching catalyst is designed to help us overcome our unrealistic restraints, fears, penetrate non-existent boundaries, speculate and think big. It helps us expand our consciousness, think the unthinkable and impossible, and thereby clear the cobwebs from our minds. "A man's mind, stretched by a new idea, can never go back to its original dimension," wrote Oliver Wendell Holmes.

Science fiction writing tends to stretch the mind of man to stimulate new achievements in science. Inventor Charles F. Kettering often stretched the minds of himself and those around him. At a time when General Motors was spending about 17 days to paint each car, he proposed to a group of his fellow researchers to paint them in one hour. No one congratulated him on his idea, rather they snickered. It did seem ridiculous. However, in a few months he achieved that goal. The elimination approach used by Procter and Gamble Corporation strives to eliminate the cost of something completely and is a mind stretching approach, which often leads to good cost savings through partial elimination of cost.

Abraham Maslow, in his book Eupsychian Management, wrote that he has always felt that motivated, creative people have had a special genius of some sort which has nothing to do with the health of the personality. ". . . just plain hard work, for one thing, and for another, just plain nerve; for example, like someone who arbitrarily defines himself as an artist in a nervy and arrogant way and therefore is an artist because he treats himself like an artist, everybody tends to also." Mind Stretching requires the nervy stretch of the problem, qoals and objectives.

To Mind Stretch, first list the goals, objectives and/or criteria which the solution of the problem is to satisfy. Then, stretch each goal, objective or criterion and write down any ideas which are stimulated. The following examples are intended to clarify this catalyst and provide a format for its use.

Problem: To design a better soda pop can.

Design objectives: The can should be economical, simple, easy to open, occupy little space, easy to store and attractive.

Original Design Objectives	Stretched Objectives	Possible Solution Ideas Stimulated
Economical.	No cost.	Returnable cans or cans which can later be used as cups.
Simple.	Very simple.	A cylindrical can with screw top.
Easy to open.	Opens by itself.	When the can touches the mouth, lip pressure on a key spot opens the container.
Occupies little space.	No space is wasted.	Square cans.

-125-

Original Design Objectives	Stretched Objectives	Possible Solution Ideas Stimulated
Easy to store after being opened.	Need not be refrigerated.	Design vacuum tight cans with resealing capability.
Attractive.	A decorator's delight.	Have advertisement on top and bottom. Have various art works printed on the visible sides of cans.

The objective of an economical can design was stretched to suggest a design which costs nothing. It is unlikely that a zero cost can could be designed. However, this initial unreasonable stretching of objective may lead to a new, not zero cost, but less costly design. We may not have even considered these design possibilities if we didn't take a few moments to "think big" by mind stretching.

Not all of these solution ideas will lead to an economical, simple, easy to open and attractive soda pop can. However, some of them may. Even if no practical ideas result, we have for a moment expanded and stretched our mind, providing it with a view of fresh possibilities which may later lead to usable creative ideas. Another example of Mind Stretch follows:

Problem: What things can I do to help me get an "A" in a History course?

Solution objectives: My solution should require little effort on my part, be low cost and help me grow mentally.

Original Design Objectives	Stretched Objectives	Possible Solution Ideas Stimulated
Little effort.	No effort.	Study with friends or make study a social occasion so that it's, in effect, effortless.

Original Design Objectives	Stretched Objectives	Possible Solution Ideas Stimulated
Low cost.	Get paid.	Try to develop an article on history for a magazine or work as a history teacher's aide.
Mental growth.	Become as knowledgeable as my teacher.	Study beyond the book and lectures. Ask many questions.

The stretched objectives--no effort from little effort, get paid from low cost, as knowledgeable as my teacher from mental growth--are nervy and far-fetched. However, the possible solution ideas, such as study with a friend or try to write a news article, are reasonable possibilities that you may not have considered if you hadn't Mind Stretched. A third example of Mind Stretch follows:

Problem: In what ways can I become more physically fit?

Original Solution Objective	Stretched Objectives	Possible Solution Ideas Stimulated
Little time required.	No time required.	Use isometric exercises while riding in a car pool or sitting in meettings, walk fast between appointments or stand when you could sit.
Little cost.	No cost.	Jog or do other exercises which involve no equipment. Jog during lunch and save money or
	Or make money.	start exercise club and charge other members.

Original Solution Objective	Stretched Objectives	Possible Solution Ideas Stimulated
Short period of time.	Immediately.	Sleep and eat better tonight.
Little change in diet.	No change in diet.	Eat foods with similar taste to those in present diet but that are more nutritious or eat less of the same food.

Objectives, goals and criteria which relate to problem solutions arise from cost factors, time and timing factors, effect on existing people and/or equipment, moral and legal factors, and personal repercussions if a failure occurs. Cost factors include capital cost (initial out-of-the-pocket costs) and operating costs (costs to keep things going).

If we choose tennis as a sport to help us get physically fit, we encounter the capital costs of a racket, clothes, shoes and possible club membership. Operating costs of tennis balls, restringing rackets, and replacing worn out shoes and clothes are encountered. Time factors, with respect to tennis, include how long each day or week must I play to keep fit and proficient. Timing factors include when do I have free time to play, when do potential playing partners have free time to play and when are courts available. The moral and legal factors relating to tennis are not significant (for amateurs). The effect on existing people might be the negative effect on your families or friends if you are less available to be with them. However, this may be offset by the positive effect of being more vigorous and alert while around them. If you fail, if tennis doesn't help you get physically fit, you only lose a small investment of time and money and can try something else.

Mind Stretch helps us think big for a minute by stretching the goals and objectives which we desire our problem solution to achieve. This "stretch" leads to creative, fresh solution ideas and stimulates our mind in an unhabitual way.

Creativity Grows with Exercise! (Mind Stretch)

Solution to the nine dot problem:

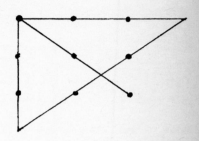

1. Discuss the following statements:
   a. "Educated people should not take their education too seriously if they want to be an inventor."   Charles F. Kettering
   b. Most of us are too conservative in our initial production of solution ideas for a problem.
   c. "A man's mind, stretched by a new idea, can never go back to its original dimensions."   Oliver Wendell Holmes
2. List as many objectives, criteria or goals as you can to draw a boundary around possible solutions for the following problems:
   a. Design a collapsible bicycle.
   b. In what ways can I be better to my friends?
   c. In what ways can this book be improved?
3. Use the Mind Stretch catalyst to provide ideas for the solution to the following problems. List at least three solution objectives and solution ideas for each problem. Use the format used in the

Mind Stretch example problems.

a. Design a better toothpaste dispenser.

b. Design a better mouse trap.

c. In what ways can I improve my reading comprehension?

d. In what ways can I dress better?

e. In what ways can we save electrical energy in our homes?

4. Use Mind Stretch to obtain creative solution ideas for the problems in exercise 2.

Chapter 8

OPEN YOURSELF TO MANY DIVERSE IDEAS

Creative problem solvers collect many ideas before they identify the best idea. They are not like "ordinary" people who, once a good idea or feasible method is found, either pursue it to completion or fail in the process before they consider another idea. If they feel it is necessary to "keep the boss happy," they will develop a list of alternative ideas to choose from in addition to their original idea to show their boss that they are creative and have considered many alternative ideas, even though they still plan to use their first idea.

John Dewey observed, "An idea is a method of evading, circumventing, or surmounting through reflections obstacles that otherwise would have to be attacked by brute force." If we constantly grasp and hold onto the first idea that we produce, we may have to use a "big hammer" to make the idea work. The further along we take a poor idea, the bigger the hammer we must use to make it work. The big hammer may be in the form of more and more money, people, time and/or energy. To avoid this primitive, but often used approach to problem solving, we must develop a large number of different ideas before we select the best idea to provide us with a greater chance of success. This helps open our minds to many diverse ideas, to see things which others often overlook, to see contrast between ideas, view ideas from different perspectives and to compare ideas.

Creative people such as Vincent Van Gogh and Linus Pauling got their best ideas after developing many good ideas (quality from quantity). The more we seek and are open to ideas, the more creative we become. Ideas may come from many sources: other people, reading, observing and our unconscious mind. All ideas should be considered. As Winston Churchill wrote, "No idea is so outlandish that it should not be considered with a searching but at the same time steady eye."

I once proposed an idea for improving the curriculum of a college to its president. He was open and receptive to the idea. However, before I was able to discuss the details of my proposals, he questioned, "In what other ways might we achieve a similar or better improvement to the curriculum?" We discussed several alternatives but finally agreed on my original proposal. This pattern of being open to alternative ideas and encouraging the consideration of many ideas is a major asset of this college president. He felt that you always have the first idea and can return to it if subsequent ideas are judged to be inferior. On the other hand, there is a good chance that subsequent ideas may be much better than the first one.

During the open phase of problem solving, don't worry about details and specifics. Delay judgment. Wait until the Identify stage. Consider your preliminary ideas as seeds. Not all seeds produce trees and not all trees bear fruit. However, the more seeds you plant, the greater is your chance of a fruitful harvest. Remember that the average gold miner must dig up about four tons of ore to produce one ounce of gold.

The Mind Prompt, Mind Surprise, Mind Free and Mind Synthesize creativity catalysts are tools to help us develop a large number of diverse idea seeds. Mind Prompt helps us tap the resources of other people for ideas. Mind Surprise and Mind Free help us break our own habitual ways of producing ideas and tap our unconscious mind for ideas. Mind Synthesize helps us combine existing ideas to produce new ideas.

Using Idea Prompters (Mind Prompt)

The writer, Henry James, obtained the idea seed for his novel,
The Spoils of Poynton, during a casual discussion with a neighbor who
unwittingly dropped it as a "mere floating particle in the stream of
talk." He felt that stray suggestions and wandering words often touch
the novelist's imagination and may provide the seed for a new novel.

The mind prompting catalyst is a deliberate effort, as opposed
to Henry James's accidental prompting by his neighbor, to seek idea
prompters or seeds from other people with diverse backgrounds, knowledge,
and intelligence. The idea prompters can come from other people's writing, conversation or products. Seeking ideas from others provides us
with another set of eyes, experiences and memories. And sometimes they
are able to see some trees in our forest. We are able to learn from
their mistakes.

Joe Paterno, the fourth winningest college football coach of all
time, is not too proud to seek coaching ideas from others. Even late
in his career, at age forty-nine, he visited other football team coaches
to rejuvenate himself and his coaching. "You better not be afraid to go
to others and say, 'What are you doing?' You better not be afraid to
ask questions or you're in trouble," remarked Paterno.

Industrial organizations, governments, and universities often spend
millions of dollars for advice from consultants and research, which in
effect constitutes an organized way to ask other people for problem-solving help. A false sense of pride often prevents many of us as individuals from utilizing the resources of others.

Not only is Mind Prompting a productive way of tapping the resources
of others, it is a simple enjoyable means of obtaining creative ideas.

Every discussion or conversation with other people offers an opportunity
to obtain prompters for good ideas.

Mind prompting stresses using conversation with people who <u>don't</u> have
experience or knowledge in your area of problem solving as a stimulus for
your creative ideas. For example, a businessman might ask his children
for ideas related to a business venture, or an educator might ask a plumb-
er for ideas on teaching. The ideas provided are not clean, finished or
necessarily directly usable ideas, but they may prompt or stimulate new
directions of thinking and lead to good creative ideas of our own. Each
time we talk with someone, their ideas may prompt our own ideas (see illustration 21).

Mind Prompting
Illustration 21

One of my students was trying to develop a visual approach to pre-senting information she was preparing for a lecture. She asked a child who suggested that she "put legs on it." This apparently worthless sug-gestion prompted my student to consider the incorporation of movement into her visual material. She finally decided to present the visual in-formation on large sheets of cardboard arranged in an artistic mobile. The mobile moved enough in the air to attract attention but yet was steady enough to be easily read. Mr. Clarence Birdseye observed the Eskimo's approach to quickly freezing food. This acted as a prompter for the frozen-food industry which he founded.

I used mind prompting to gain new ideas for and fresh insights into the problem, "In what ways can I use my time at work most effectively?" A seven year old child I asked said, "Eat less." This prompted me to consider using mealtimes to discuss important matters with others, a practice often used by businessmen. A housewife I asked recommended that I do my hardest work in the morning. This thought prompted me to consider working during the time of the day when I work most effective-ly, which is in the afternoon. I asked a businessman, who suggested that the setting of completion deadlines increases the amount of work accomplished. This suggestion is a direct value "as is" for my prob-lem. Note that most of the ideas suggested were not taken "as is" but were used as prompters for my own ideas--ideas which fit my unique needs and capabilities. When the child recommended that I eat less, this prompted a similar but distinctly different idea in my mind--use mealtimes to discuss important matters with others.

Recommendations by obviously unknowledgeable sources such as small children are generally considered to be unfactual and should only be considered as a prompter for our own ideas. Unfortunately once something is written or spoken by an "authority" we often consider it to be a fact. As a young man, I once challenged the pastor of our church with a fact that I had found in a book. I implied that books don't lie. His reply was that, while books don't "lie" (are not in error), the writers of books often do. Errors in the written and spoken word are frequent. Some errors are corrected, but others, even those which are not consistent with the facts of everyday experience, are widely accepted as gospel. Many books have listed and classified errors. Here are some errors which have been published in books: Abraham Lincoln jotted down the Gettysburg Address on the back of an envelope while he was going to Gettysburg. Wrong! He worked on it for several weeks. Even after he had made the speech, but before it was published, he made further changes in the text of the speech. Galileo climbed the Tower of Pisa and dropped two cannonballs of different weights to disprove Aristotle's theory that heavier bodies fall faster. Wrong! This never occurred.

One technical manager informally "checked out" how many times people speaking authoritatively were actually right. He estimated that most of the people he evaluated were actually only correct about 65% of the time. This doesn't mean that everyone is lying. We all have faulty memories, hear and read incorrect facts from others, and color communications with our own feelings. Therefore, even books should be considered as prompters for our own ideas, not as a source for absolutely correct ideas.

Uncertain and perhaps unfactual information from other people can be transformed into good ideas by mind prompting. To mind prompt most effectively and provide a record for other people, the following format is suggested. The problem considered is, "What new features should be offered in homes of the future?"

Source	Prompter	Possibly Usable Idea
Engineer	A master control for the lights located in the kitchen.	A master control for lights and temperature located in the master bedroom.
5-year-old child	Drinking fountain in the bedroom.	A drinking fountain in the bathroom.
Housewife	Dustless house.	Powerful filters which remove dust from the air continuously.

Note that the prompter ideas were used as triggers or stimulators for possible good ideas rather than as ideas to be accepted or rejected "as is." What is prompted in our mind depends largely on what we know and what is important to us. The recommendation by a Boxer to improve pencils by making them easier to "hold on to" would prompt different usable ideas for different people. In a writer's mind, it might prompt the idea for a cushioned pencil which would be easier to hold on to for long periods of time. In a mechanic's mind, it might prompt the idea for a pencil which doesn't slip in greasy hands.

Synectics Inc. often purposefully integrates individuals with diverse backgrounds and capabilities into the problem-solving process. This produces a cross-prompting effect where poor or incomplete ideas from one individual may provide the source for a good idea for someone else.

Edison believed that he got some of his ideas from a source outside himself. Once, when he was complimented for a creative idea, he disclaimed credit saying, "Ideas are in the air" and if he had not discovered it, someone else would have. Ideas are "in the air" but we won't see them if we don't open ourselves to prompters from other people, literature and observation. These ideas may lead us to break habitual ways of perceiving and to ultimately gain fresh insights and develop original ideas. "Genius, in truth, means little more than the faculty of perceiving in an unhabitual way," wrote William James.

Patents for "transmitting sounds telegraphically" were filed on the same day in the U.S. Patent Office by Alexander Graham Bell, of Salem, Massachusetts and Elisha Gray, of Chicago, Illinois. Bell finally was awarded the patent. Simultaneous, or near-simultaneous, inventions and discoveries often occur when ideas are "in the air." Many of us don't profit from the ideas that are "in the air" because we only accept complete, finished, practical solutions from others for our problems. We are not properly "tuned-in" to the idea seeds and prompters which abound in our environment.

Mind Prompting can be used for any type of problem. Consider the problem, "Invent a better pencil." Using the mind prompting format suggested earlier, the following possible usable ideas were prompted:

Source	Prompter	Possibly Usable Ideas
Secretary	A pencil which can't be lost.	Make pencils that are extra long.
Teacher	A pencil which stays sharp.	Try to develop harder leads or a rotating lead that "self-sharpens."
Teenager	A cheap pencil.	This is a good design goal "as is."
Boxer	A pencil which is easy to hold on to.	Roughen the surface of the pencil so that it is easier to grip.

When seeking ideas from others, don't simply look for support of your existing ideas by phrasing your questions as, "Don't you think..." or "Don't you agree...?" Rather, ask an open question like, "What do you think..." We are always in danger of listening to and believing only those people who have the good sense to agree with us and think as we think.

Discussing a problem with others not only prompts new ideas, it helps us define the problem in our own mind. It may well develop a new viewpoint or approach to its solution. Many of us have experienced having the answer to a question drop into our mind the moment we began to ask the question. Often students raise their hand, begin to ask a question, then say, "Never mind, I understand now," even before the teacher has a chance to hear the question. I have often wondered if people might not be able to obtain many answers to their problems by asking some imaginary person. The very act of articulating the question might stimulate good answers, or at least clarify the problem.

No one stops eating at age 21, but starved imaginations are common-place. As we get older, some people stop asking questions and reading a variety of books. As Charles P. Steinmetz observed, there are no foolish questions and no man becomes a fool until he has stopped asking questions.

Don't just sit around waiting for ideas and inspirations. Collect all of the facts, information and ideas related to your problem that time allows. Observe, read, travel and talk to other people. This data you collect becomes valuable only if you are open to it and use it for what it is worth. That is, use anything other than verifiable facts as prompters for ideas of your own. The creative way is to utilize any and all input, even poor input, as possible prompters or seeds for your own creative ideas.

Creativity Grows With Exercise!

1. Observe and/or question several people you consider to be effective and creative. Do they seek the ideas of other people? Do they treat the ideas of others as facts? Write a one-page paper discussing your observations.

2. Define a problem of your choice. Then, thumb through a catalogue such as Sears or the advertisements in a magazine. Try to use this reading to prompt a minimum of three inventions or business ideas of your own.

3. Define a problem (any problem). Ask three children under ten years of age what solutions they can think of for your problem. What good ideas of your own did they prompt? Write a brief discussion of your results.

4. Mind Prompting is similar to the process of word association. Randomly pick three words from the dictionary. Try to use them to prompt, through word association, ideas for the problem: How can I enjoy life more?

5. List at least three ways you could get prompting ideas from your friends for the solution to a problem without their knowing that you are seeking their help.

6. Ask three people the percentage of the time they think that they and others are correct in their statements.

7. Problem: In what ways can the design of a can opener be improved? Try to transform the prompters into possibly good solutions to this problem.

Source	Prompter	Transformed Possibly Good Ideas
Five-year-old child.	Make it easier.	Keep design simple
Stranger met on bus.	Make them easy to find.	enough for a child
Mechanic.	Make them long lasting.	to use.
Housewife.	Make them easier to clean.	
Engineering student.	Use an electrical drive.	

8. Problem: In what ways can we become better listeners? Ask the next three people you encounter for several solutions to the problem stated. Use these ideas as prompters for your own ideas.

Source	Prompter	Transformed Possibly Good Ideas

9. Use mind prompting with a format like that used in exercises 7 and 8 to provide new ideas for, and fresh insights into, the following problems. For each problem use at least three different people as prompters.

a. Determine as many uses as you can for worn-out car tires.

b. In what ways should elementary schools be improved?

c. In what ways can we help low-income people eat well?

d. List the titles of several new books which you feel should be written.

e. Design a screwdriver head which won't slip off the screw.

Using Wild Ideas (Mind Surprise)

Abraham H. Maslow observed that every really new idea looks crazy at first. Alfred North Whitehead wrote, "Almost all really new ideas have a certain aspect of foolishness when they are just produced." So why not try to intentionally, deliberately generate crazy, foolish, wild ideas as a strategy to catalyze new, fresh, good ideas and insights.

Creativity in adults often arises from sources similar to the play of children. Mind Surprising helps us tap this playfulness in each of us and transform it into practical results. The mental associations and stimulation which result from "playing" with strange, far-out ideas often lead to novel and original solutions to a problem.

Although it is difficult to be playful and temporarily silly, these are important keys to releasing ideas. Originality results from being adventuresome and taking the risk of saying or writing down whatever idea enters your mind, no matter how wild or silly the idea seems. Brainstorming groups actually prize "far-out," strange and silly ideas because often they can be modified or transformed into excellent usable ideas. One research study found that a large percentage of all "far-out" ideas produced can be transformed into good practical ideas.

From a list of ridiculous, laughable ideas, it is sometimes possible to pick the seemingly silliest and transform it into the best idea of all. In any event, the mental associations that result from playing with these silly ideas often stimulate good ideas. Silly, laughable, ridiculous ideas for using an old brick include: using it as a toy boat, playing catch with it or using it as a hat. These laughable ideas for brick usage may stimulate good, fairly reasonable ideas if we work to transform them into reasonable ideas. The idea playing catch with it might trigger

the idea of using a brick as a door stop (catch). The laughable idea
of using a "brick as a hat" might trigger the possibly good idea of
building a unique hat rack out of bricks.

Mind Surprising may be considered by some people as a sure way
to get fired or lose face. Perhaps it is a sure way to get fired if
the laughable ideas aren't ultimately transformed into possibly usable
ideas. We must continually remind ourselves that many great ideas were
first greeted with sneers and critical reactions. However, often laughable ideas may in fact be good ideas. The steamboat was initially called
"Fulton's Folly."

Mind Surprise was used in the following example to stimulate fresh
ideas for the solutions to, and insights into, the problem, "In what
ways can I make more friends?"

Ridiculous, laughable ideas:	Transformed, possibly good ideas:
Scream a lot.	Let people know you are around (tactfully).
Kick people.	Don't hurt people's feelings.
Eat a lot.	Invite people over for, or out to, lunch.
Sweat a lot.	Making friends takes a lot of work.

Mind Surprise provides fresh insights into problems as well as new
ideas for their solution. The laughable idea of making friends by "kick-
ing people" was transformed into the possibly good idea of not hurting
people's feelings. On the other hand, the laughable idea of sweating a
lot to gain friends was transformed into the fresh insight that making
friends requires a lot of work.

When using Mind Surprise, it is very important to list all wild ideas first, then transform them one at a time into possibly good ideas.

In the following problems, the Mind Surprise technique was used to stimulate fresh ideas for the problem, "In what ways can I protect my home from burglars?" First, laughable and ridiculous ideas were listed. Then they were transformed into good, possibly usable ideas and insights.

Ridiculous, laughable ideas:	Transformed, possibly good ideas:
Use trained alligators.	Use trained dogs.
Build a moat around the house.	Build a fence around the house.
Leave all windows open.	Make house look lived-in.
Notify burglars when you are leaving.	Notify police and neighbors when you are leaving.

Have fun - Mind Surprise! Remember, creativity in adults arises from sources similar to the play of children. It involves first playing with ridiculous, laughable ideas in a child-like fashion, then being an adult and transforming your play into surprisingly good results. Creativity is looking at something and seeing something else. Creatively examining and playing with ridiculous, laughable ideas and finding good, usable ideas is a creative achievement. Try it. You will surprise yourself with the good ideas and fresh insights you develop.

Creativity Grows With Exercise!
(In each of these exercises, use the format used in the Mind Surprising examples.)

1. Use five mind surprising or laughable ideas to prompt good ideas for the problem: "In what ways can I entertain a young child in the car during a long trip if no toys, book, papers or pencils are available?"

2. Use mind surprising to help list as many ideas as you can, in five

minutes, for uses of a wire coat hanger.

3. Seek at least five ridiculous, laughable ideas from other people on the problem used in exercise two. When asking for ideas, stress that you only want wild, ridiculous or laughable ideas. Try to transform these ideas into reasonable ideas.

4. Develop possibly good ideas and fresh insights into the problem, "In what ways can I find a new friend?" Use the silly, laughable ideas provided as triggers for your own possibly good ideas.

Ridiculous, laughable ideas:	Transformed, possibly good ideas:
Work hard.	
Eat fish.	
Faint.	
Spit on cars.	

5. List a minimum of ten ideas for the solution to the following problems. If you run out of ideas, use Mind Surprise to help you develop more ideas.

   a. In what ways can I study better?

   b. In what ways can I make more money?

   c. In what ways can I help more people?

   d. In what ways can energy be conserved in a house?

   e. What are some possible new ideas for children's toys?

   f. What are some innovative ways in which pencils could be sharpened?

6. List a minimum of fifteen ideas for the solution to any three problems of your choice. Use Mind Surprising to stimulate at least half the ideas.

7. Explain, through discussion and example, the Mind Surprising

technique to three people. Write a few sentences about the reaction
of each person to the Mind Surprising technique.

8. Draw a picture which you feel captures the essence of the Mind Surprising techniques.

9. Write a poem which you feel captures the essence of the Mind Surprising
technique.

Using Similarities (Mind Free)

Sometimes we feel that to be creative or original requires isolating
yourself from those around you. If you do, be careful, because you may
end up reinventing the wheel. Determine the current state of art and how
other people have solved problems similar to yours before you select your
best idea. If your problem is to design a container for drinking glasses,
check with other designers or companies to see how they have already solved
the problem of packing delicate items. Use their ideas "as is" or as
stimulators for your own ideas. If your problem is how to get a higher
salary, ask your friends or read relevant literature to determine how
others have approached similar problems.

To be a little more creative, use problems which aren't exactly the
same as yours to stimulate new ideas. In the packing problem, you might
consider packing glasses as similar analogies to packing animals for
shipment, packing explosives or the packing of any delicate item as a
source of stimulation. In the case of trying to obtain a higher salary,
you might use the problems of how to get promoted, how to win friends or
another related problem as an analogy to your problem to stimulate ideas
which relate to your own problem.

We tend to be locked into fixed habitual ways of "looking" at things
and interpreting words. To get a better feel for this reality, try the

following problem. You have been hired, as a landscaper, to plant five rows of trees with four trees in each row. Your employer wants you to do this with only a total of ten trees. The solution is located at the end of this section.

One of the primary inhibitors to solving the tree problem is our fixed, habitual vision of relationship between trees and rows, and the idea of counting each tree only once. Mind Freeing is a creative technique designed to help us "see" things and relationships between things in different fresh ways and to use our habitual way of looking at things as an advantage rather than a hindrance. Other habitual relationships include ham and eggs, pen and paper, school and books, and car and road.

Often seemingly unrelated things in nature can provide insights into, and solutions for, the problems of man. The honeycomb design of beehives may have provided the stimulus for the honeycomb design of many high-strength, low-weight panels used for engineering designs. Fish fins may have led to the development of swim fins, birds' nests to thatched roofs, octopus arms to suction cups, bats' sensing to radar, porpoise sleakness to submarines, rattlesnake sensing to infrared sensing, and rattlesnake fangs to hypodermic needles.

The bird obviously provided a basis for the design of airplanes (see illustration 22). Many similarities exist between birds and airplanes. However, even more dissimilarities exist. For example, airplanes don't flap their wings and don't have feathers. Some early and short-lived airplane designers insisted on the use of feathers for their air machines and flapping as a means of propulsion. They used the bird as a prescription for airplane design rather than a stimulus for their own design ideas. Even today, man cannot build an exact replica of bird feathers, let alone an entire bird. The creative person uses analogies, metaphors or similar objects as stimulus triggers or seeds for ideas; not as prescription for them. They use many diverse items which they encounter as analogies to trigger new visions of what could be solutions to their problem.

An Analogy
Illustration 22

Oftentimes, even seemingly completely unrelated things can provide stimuli for the solution to a problem. Leonardo da Vinci remarked, "I cannot forbear to mention...a new device for study which, although it may seem trivial and almost ludicrous, is nevertheless extremely useful in arousing the mind to various inventions. And this is, when you look at a wall spotted with stains...you may discover a resemblance to various

landscapes, beautified with mountains, rivers, rocks, trees...or again
you may see battles and figures in action, or strange faces and cos-
tumes, and an endless variety of objects which you could reduce to complete and well-drawn forms. And these appear on such walls confusedly,
like the sound of bells in whose jangle you may find any name or word
you choose to imagine."

On the surface, the similarity of a wall spotted with stains and
beautiful mountains, rivers and streams is remote. However, if we cul-
tivate our creative imagination, we can find similarities between any
two things and stimulate our own creativity in the process. What are
the similarities between a blade of grass and a kitchen knife? What
ideas for the design of a new kitchen knife can we obtain from a blade
of grass? Grass is green, has roots, is somewhat waterproof and it
grows. The fact that grass is green might lead us to design colored
knives; grass roots might lead to the idea of a holder, snap or leash
attached to a knife to keep it rooted (from leaving) to the kitchen
area. The fact that water tends to roll off grass may lead to the
idea of a surface finish on a knife which repels water. The fact that
grass grows might lead us to design a telescoping or collapsible knife.

To make grass similar to a kitchen knife requires the use of
creative imagination. It requires making something relevant that is
not normally considered relevant. Wm. J. J. Gordon, the father of
Synectics approach to creativity, observed that everything is relevant
and that making things relevant is the creative process.

To imagine similarities between ideas which seem unrelated according to our habitual ways of associating things, we must force relationships; i.e., deliberately and purposely relate attributes of one

seemingly unrelated item to that of another. Grass was "forced" to be similar to a kitchen knife.

A doughnut can be forced to be similar to a shoe. A doughnut is round. Most edges on shoes are round. A doughnut has a hole which goes through it. Some shoes provide holes in their surface to aerate the foot. Doughnuts contain air pockets. Some shoes are designed with foam-like airy soles for comfort.

To be deliberate and creative problem solvers, we must not only force relationships between unrelated items, we must force new and original relationships which may lead to new creative problem solutions. Creative thinking is looking at something and seeing something else. The Mind Freeing techniques for stimulating new ideas provide us with a method for the deliberate examination of something and imagining similarities to other things. This procedure often results in fresh insights and new ideas.

To Mind Free:

1. Arbitrarily choose a physical object, picture, plant or animal. The more remote your choice is from the problem, the greater the chance will be that a creative idea or fresh insight will be stimulated.

2. List the characteristics of the chosen item in detail. Be sure to complete step 2 before beginning step 3.

3. Free your mind creativity with new ideas and insights by forcing similarities between your problem and the attributes of the item you arbitrarily chose.

An example of Mind Freeing applied to the problem, "What is creative thinking?" follows. A staircase shell sketched on the following page was chosen as an imagined likeness or analogy to creative thinking.

A Staircase Shell

Attributes of a Staircase Shell	Imagined Similarity to Creative Thinking
Spiral	Creative thinking is not a straight line process, but requires intense focus.
From nature	Creative thinking is inherent to the nature of man.
Hard	Creative thinking conquers even the hardest problem.
Shell (empty inside)	Creative thinking helps to penetrate the shell of human existence.
Circular	Creative thinking is a continuous process.
One Opening	Non-creative thinking produces only one idea.
Looks like a spring	Creative thinking is flexible thinking. The more thinking is stretched creatively, the greater is the potential energy of the creative thought.
Hypnotic design	Creative thinking consumes people.
Expansive looking	Creative thinking expands the mind.
Wide open	Creative thinking is open to all.
Beautiful (natural)	Thinking is part of the beautiful nature of man.

In this example, the attributes of the physical object--staircase shell--stimulated fresh insights into the problem, "What is creative thinking?" Many of the insights stimulated in this example, such as creative thinking is a continuous process, are fairly obvious but may not be recalled without the Mind Freeing stimulus. Other insights, such as creative thinking helps to penetrate the shell of human existence, may be new thoughts, or at least present fresh approaches to old thoughts.

Mind Freeing was used to help develop fresh ideas for, and insights into, the problem, "How can a better single family residence be designed?" A pencil was used as likeness to a single family residence to free the mind from habitual thinking.

Attributes of a Pencil	Imagined Similarity to a Single Family Residence
Lead in center	Utilities could be located in center of the home.
Eraser on one end	The end of home, which is recreation oriented, should be easy to clean.
Hexagonal	A hexagonally shaped home might be of interest.
Pointed	A roof with a steep pitch might be considered.
Metal band	Use some metal for the exterior of the house. Perhaps a metal sculpture could be placed on a front wall.
Made of wood	Houses are usually made of wood.
Painted gold	Paint the house a rich, bright and cheery color.

What is the similarity between a woodpecker and a football player? The similarity used for a 1976 research project was that they both receive severe jolts to their heads frequently. Researchers at UCLA and the Veterans Administration studied the woodpecker's head structure to find better ways of designing football helmets. In woodpeckers they found dense, spongy bone, tightly packing a narrow brain with relatively little fluid to transmit shock and encircled by shock-absorbing muscles. The conclusion of the researchers was that football helmets might be improved by the use of a lighter, thicker, form-fitting, firm but spongy helmet with a relatively thin and hard outer shell to protect against abrasion.

These researchers looked at something (a woodpecker's head), and saw something else (a football helmet). William James stated that high creativity comes with an ability for "similarity association." The approach these researchers used was creative and is an example of the Mind Freeing catalyst.

The following example uses Mind Freeing to develop insights into the problem, "How can I use my time more effectively?" A hawk was chosen for use as an analogy.

Attributes of a Hawk	Imagine Similarities to Using Your Time Effectively
Feathers	Time can float away if deadlines aren't established.
Talons	Grab the time you have while driving a car and waiting for appointments with others and use it purposefully.
Flies and perches	Plan time for rest and recreation as well as work.
Dives quickly	When you spot your prey (important matters) act swiftly on them.
Good eye vision	Allow time for long-term planning (making visions) into the future.

Mind Freeing not only helps us be creative in our approach to the problem solving, it helps us become more creative by becoming more aware of our environment. We observe the fine points of hawks, pencils and shells more perceptively. Synectics Incorporated uses analogies and metaphors as their principle problem solving as well as a teaching

-153-

tool. For example, they might use a volcano as a metaphor or analogy to discuss the revolution in Cuba. The molten subterranean lava may represent the revolutionaries. The mountain, the established government, and so on. The students gain from a discussion such as this in several ways; they understand volcanos better, revolution better and have a tool for helping them remember what they learned.

Writers often use analogy to underscore ideas, provide format to concepts and tease the mind: Love is like a flower, Man is the salt of the earth, and Vice is like a spider web.

Solution to Tree Problem (page 147):

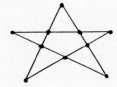

Creativity Grows With Exercise!

1. List several animals which might be logical analogies to a vacuum cleaner.

2. In what ways is an ant similar to an office worker?

3. "A child is like an unfolding flower; it is fresh and vibrant." Complete the following in a similar fashion:

   "A mind is like a safe; it is _____."

   "Our creativity is like popcorn; it is _____."

   "Love is like a _____; _____."

   "Problem solving is like a _____; _____."

   "Habit is like a _____; _____."

"College is like _____; _____."

4. What do the following have in common?:

    a. Day and egg.

    b. Horse and car.

    c. Men and dogs.

    d. Light bulb and education.

    e. Octopus and can opener.

    f. Fish and purse.

    g. Warfare and courtship.

    h. Freeway system and human circulatory system.

    i. Basketball and mountain climbing.

    j. Business and college.

    k. Magnet and food.

5. What are the differences which exist between the pairs of words in exercise 4?

6. Using an ant as an analogy, list as many ideas as you can for improving the efficiency of factory workers.

7. Use a pencil as an analogy to force ideas for the design of a single family residence. (This problem was initiated earlier in this chapter.)

Attributes of a Pencil	Imagined Similarities to a Single Family Residence
Eraser is red. Long and narrow. Must be sharpened. Function properly. Held in hand. Light weight.	

8. Use, as an analogy, how a Kangaroo packages her baby to how to package glasses as a way to free new ideas for packaging.

Attributes of a Kangaroo Pouch	Imagined Similarity to Packaging Glasses
For example, a pouch is soft.	Use a packing material such as foam rubber.
For example, one opening.	Stack glasses in long, cylindrical containers.
For example, flexible, attached to stomach, cozy and comfortable.	Design container to fold up when not in use.
(Add a few attributes of your own.)	

9. Design an improved can opener for pop cans using the steps for Mind Freeing which follow. Develop at least seven ideas or insights.
   a. Arbitrarily choose a physical object, picture or animal.
   b. List its characteristics in detail.
   c. Surprise your mind with new ideas and insights by imagining similarities between your problem and the attributes of the item you arbitrarily chose as a likeness to your challenge.

Attribute of	Imagined Similarities to

10. Write a one-page story on love using a flower as an analogy for love.

11. Imagine that you are a Martian who has just landed on earth. Your first contact with our civilization is a football game. What fresh insights about man does this imagined experience stimulate?

Using Synthesis (Mind Synthesize)

A camper is the combination or synthesis of a car and a home. A wheelchair is the synthesis of wheels and a chair. The synthesis of a radio and a clock results in a clock radio. The common lead pencil is a synthesis of a pencil and an eraser (see Illustration 23). Laurel and Hardy, Sonny and Cher, Jerry Lewis and Dean Martin were successful creative combinations in the entertainment field. A good basketball team is a creative synthesis of players with different heights, strengths and abilities. Many people believe that all creativity is simple; a combination or synthesis of existing elements or attributes into a new combination. Creative thinking might be considered the synthesis of ideas into a new combination where the whole of the new identity is more than the sum of its parts.

Combinations played an important role in the creations of the mathematician, Henri Poincare, as evidenced by his description of the origination of one of his creations. "For fifteen days I strove to prove that there could not be any functions like those I have since called Fuchsian functions. I was then very ignorant; every day I seated myself at my work table, stayed an hour or two, tried a great number of combinations and reached no results. One evening, contrary to my custom, I drank black coffee and could not sleep. Ideas arose in crowds. I felt them collide until pairs interlocked, so to speak, making a stable combination. By the next morning, I had established the existence of a class of Fuchsian functions, those which come from the hypergeometric series; I had only to write out the results, which took but a few hours."

Industries are a synthesis of engineering, business and marketing people. Artists combine colors and shapes. Musicians combine notes and

sound intensities. Chemists and physicists combine the elements. Mind
Synthesis is a deliberate systematic creative method for the logical
and haphazard combining of ideas to produce new ideas and fresh insights.

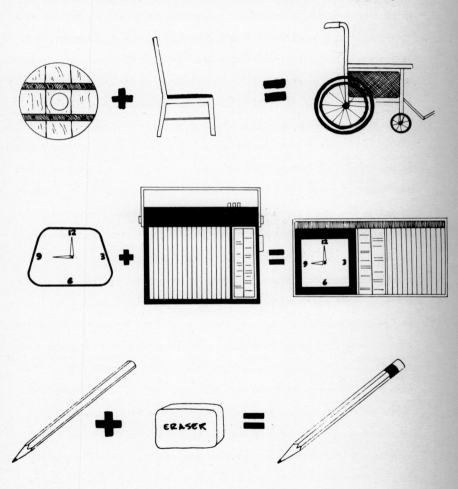

Creative Combinations
Illustration 23

A great way to produce an invention idea is to combine items which might lead to new useful ideas. In my office are a light and a desk. They logically might be combined and lead to the idea of a desk lamp, a decorative lamp base designed in the form of a desk, lights built into a desk drawer or a light built into a desk top. The desk and chair in my office could be synthesized to stimulate the idea of a chair with attached writing surface, or a desk with an attached swing-out chair. The synthesis of the pencil in my hand, and the notebook I am writing in, might lead to a notebook with a pencil on a leash or a chain.

In addition to logical combinations, random or haphazard combinations of previously, unrelated items can often be imaginately transformed into new ideas. I used random combinations of items in my office as a way to stimulate new ideas for inventions. To emphasize the randomness of the choice, I listed items in my office in two columns with six items in each column. Column 1 includes my file cabinet, desk, coffee cup, telephone, carpet and stapler. Column 2 includes my bookcase, sunglasses, a light, a clock, chair and light switch. A toss of the dice suggested the combination of the carpet and my sunglasses, which lead to the possible invention ideas with carpet-like frames, sunglass cases made from carpets or tinted windows to prevent the carpet from fading. Another role of the dice produced the combination desk and light switch. The synthesis of these two elements might lead to a switch on the desk which controls the light in the room or a desk which is locked when lights are turned out. A third roll of the dice produced the apparently unproductive combination of a comb and a book. This combination led to the idea of a device for combining a book for essential information on packaging combs for sale in book form, writing a book on the proper use of a comb, or a comb on which famous quotations are inscribed.

In the dice example, the logical and haphazard combinations were made to provide ideas for possibilities. No effort was made to apply the synthesis process to help solve a specific problem. The primary purpose of Mind Synthesis is to help produce fresh insight into new ideas for the solution of specific problems.

To apply Mind Synthesis to a problem, first list as many solution ideas for a problem as possible. Then logically and randomly combine two or more initial ideas to stimulate new creative ideas.

If our problem is to improve the design of a paper clip dispenser, possible solution ideas include a dispenser which holds more clips, a dispenser which dispenses the clips one at a time, a better-looking dispenser or a cheaper one. A cheaper dispenser which holds more clips suggests the insight that perhaps a larger clip container would increase the cost of the dispenser but reduce important costly secretarial time loading them. Combining the idea of a better-looking dispenser with one which won't tip over suggests a design with a low center of gravity; perhaps a vase shape might be appropriate. Combining a dispenser which holds more clips with one where clips can be easily loaded might suggest a large opening for clip insertion which would occur if a large paper clip dispenser is designed.

All combinations do not result in good new ideas. However, many do; and, in keeping with the main thrust of being creative, new creative ideas come from lots of ideas. Mathematically, the number of different possible combinations of two ideas is one, of three ideas is three, of four ideas is six and of five ideas is ten. As you can see, combinations of five new ideas can lead up to ten more ideas, a dramatic increase.

Consider the problem: "In what ways can I be better to other people?" Possible ideas include: be friendly, show an interest in them, help them and speak highly of them. The combination of being friendly, showing interest in them suggests perhaps participating in an activity with them which you both enjoy. "Speak highly of them" and "help them" might suggest that friends are helped when you speak highly of them or put a good word in for them with their boss, spouse or parents.

Creativity Grows With Exercise!

1. Randomly combine objects at your place of employment or college to list interesting possible ideas for inventions. For example, pencil combined with book might suggest a book with a loop on it to store a pencil.

2. Look in the want ads and/or business opportunities section in your newspaper and list interesting new professions or business opportunities which might result with the random (haphazard) combination of headings. For example, welder's service combined with telephone poles might suggest welding services to shops over the telephone. Try many combinations. This can be fun.

3. Use dice to randomly combine the following items to stimulate possible invention ideas.

   1. sand   1. wood
   2. hammer   2. axe
   3. clock   3. steel
   4. dial   4. pencil
   5. elastic   5. handle
   6. arm   6. cut

   For example, if the rolled dice indicated 4-2 (dial-axe), perhaps there is a need for axes which can be dialed to different sharpness or, better yet, supplied with a variety of heads.

4. Draw ten different things, using the following four geometric shapes; a triangle, square, rectangle, circle and straight lines. For example: A boat.

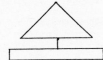

5. Name three creative combinations in each of the following areas:

    a. entertainment; example, Laurel and Hardy.

    b. art; example, black and white.

    c. music; example, quiet and loud.

    d. business; example, inventor and business capital.

6. Try to think of three items in your environment which aren't combinations of other items.

7. A couple, Walter and Helen, combined their names to create a name for one of their children, Wallen. What name would you have if your parents used a similar approach?

8. Name five apparently unproductive, uncreative, new combinations. For example: Fence and a chair, or a table and water.

9. Combine wheels with ten items in your present environment. Which of these combinations suggest new inventions? Which suggest existing inventions?

    For example: Wheels on a wastepaper basket (large ones used by janitors), stapler (might suggest new ease for sliding large stapler on desk), or desk (desks with rollers are in current use).

10. List at least five solutions to the following problems. Then

stimulate at least three new ideas by combining ideas from the original list of five or more ideas.

a. In what ways can I get the most out of this book?

b. What things might make the average pizza parlor more pleasant?

c. In what ways could the design of bicycles be improved?

d. In what ways might a mother persuade her child to keep her room clean?

e. In what ways could you, your school or business make money?

f. In what ways can a bar of soap be stored in the shower area of a bathroom?

Chapter 9

IDENTIFY THE BEST IDEA

Which is the nicest home, best food to eat, most attractive car, best approach to relations with other countries or best way to achieve success in life? These are creative problems. No one correct answer exists. The best answer is often different for each of us. One person likes a single story home, another a ranch style home, another a log cabin.

To creatively solve creative problems, problems with more than one solution, we must first carefully define the problem and develop many possible ideas for its solution. Then we must identify the best solution. The large number and great variety of ideas developed greatly enhance our efforts to obtain the best idea. However, at the same time they create a greater problem in choosing which is the best. Mind Integrate is the creative catalyst introduced in this chapter to help improve our natural approach to idea selection.

The success of the open phase of the DO IT process depends heavily on the principle of delaying judgment during the production of ideas. Even after we have chosen an idea from the list of many unpolished ideas, we must delay judgment before we try to implement our idea. We need to modify and strengthen our selected idea to make it more valuable and increase its chance of survival. Mind Strengthening is the creative catalyst we use to accomplish this goal by first viciously attacking the idea and then modifying it to make it stronger.

Mind Energizing is a creative catalyst to further modify and improve our ideas with an eye on the consequences which might result from

transforming the idea into action. It helps us modify the idea to minimize the bad consequences which might result from the implementation of
our idea and maximize the good consequences. The end result of applying
Mind Energize is a better idea and a decision as to whether or not we
should begin the process of transforming the idea into practice.

Integrating Conscious and Unconscious (Mind Integrate)

The mathematician, Henri Poincare, observed that the true work of an
inventor is to choose useful ideas from the ideas generated. He wrote
that the rules which must guide this choice are extremely fine and delicate. It is almost impossible to state them precisely. They are felt
rather than formulated. This mathematician considers feelings to be an
important part of the "objective" field of science and invention.

"Life is the art of drawing sufficient conclusions from insufficient premises," wrote Samuel Butler. Ideas are also usually selected,
based on insufficient premises and information. Enough information never
exists to draw conclusive conscious conclusions as to which idea is the
best idea. We need to draw not only on our limited conscious mind, but
also on our vast unconscious mind. Gut-level feelings, after consideration for all conscious thoughts, tend to utilize both our conscious and
unconscious mental thoughts.

Artists tend to rely exclusively (or at least think they do) on the
unconscious mind for their idea selection and decisions relating to art.
However, truly creative people capitalize on both their conscious and
their unconscious minds for the selection of the best idea. They rely on
their unique experienced knowledge and psychological and attitudinal dimensions which are stored in both their conscious and unconscious mind.

Individual Uniqueness. "Every facet of the universe, each man, woman, child, each plant and animal, the clouds and heavenly bodies, the wind and the sand and stars, each object, each space, even bits of gravel and broken stone, each item of nature, contains its own particular identity, its own unique form, its own special existence. Every aspect of nature and life contains its own spark of originality that attains a living unity and persistence of form through its relation to other identities and forms," observed Clark Moustakas in his book Creativity and Conformity. "We, like other facets of the universe, are unique and special."

Many psychologists tell us that our decision process and our ideation process are dependent on our unique psychological and experiential selves. Psychologists often use a figure like that in Illustration 24 to emphasize the effect of past experience on our perception. What do you see in this figure? Depending on your experience and current mental and psychological state, you probably see either a vase or a cocktail glass in white, or the profile of the faces of two men. (See page 168.) Try turning the figure upside down. What do you see?

Perception
Illustration 24

All that we have seen and experienced, especially those things which we have experienced successfully, become part of our mental self. We tend to choose solutions similar to those which have been successful for us in the past.

Mozart felt that his creativity was a natural result of his unique mental and psychological makeup. He related that the reason that his particular form and style is different from that of other composers is probably due to the same reason which renders his nose so large or short and different from those of other people.

Our individual uniqueness has been dramatically demonstrated to me during my college classes and workshops on creativity. To date, no two final creative projects or invention ideas developed have been the same or, in most cases, even similar.

It is ironic that, even though we often recognize and value our own uniqueness, we often don't extend this recognition to others. When people in an art gallery try to express the purpose of an artist's painting (see Illustration 25), they are usually wrong. Perhaps the artist doesn't even consciously know why he is creating a particular picture. Often the most valued works of art are those that are abstract enough to appeal to the different unique visions of many individuals. Naturalists may like a particular picture because they feel it expresses the beauty of nature. Others may like the same picture because to them it points out man's inhumanity to man.

Ours is Not to Reason Why
Illustration 25

Carl Rogers, in <u>Toward A Theory of Creativity</u>, wrote that the creative process is the emergence in action of a novel relation or product growing out of the uniqueness of the individual. To become more creative we must recognize our own uniqueness and capitalize on it by selecting ideas which we feel are of value to us based on our unique goals, needs and experience.

Gut-Level Feelings and Intuition. "Aha," "Eureka," and "It feels right" types of exclamations tend to grow out of the intuition and feelings which spring forth from our unconscious. Our intuition is not irrational and unreal, rather it is the result of unconscious mental thinking. If you feel that it will rain this afternoon, something which you are probably not consciously aware of such as the sky is cloudy, humidity is high and other times that the weather was like this it rained, is probably triggering this feeling.

Stravinsky did not feel it necessary to scientifically justify his methods. Henri Poincaré chose solutions to problems that were best able to "charm" the special sensitivity that all mathematicians know. Perhaps the most fundamental condition of creative people is their internal source of judgment and selection. The creative person listens to his inner ear more than his outer ear. This does not mean that he is oblivious to or unwilling to listen to others, or to think consciously and rationally. Rather, it means that the creative person has to "feel" it is right in addition to satisfying conscious mental conclusions.

In the "Meno," Plato argues that problem solving is simply remembering, because how else could we recognize the answer to a problem if we didn't already know it? Perhaps our feelings are really unconscious selections of answers which we already know. Whether or not Plato is correct in his argument, it is a fact that feelings are based on our accumulated knowledge and experience. If our knowledge and experience in a particular area is limited, our "gut-level feelings" in this area will be of limited value. Therefore, the "gut-level feelings" of true experts in a field are generally much more valuable and more often correct than those of amateurs.

The creative person tries to learn everything there is to know about their field or area of study before they are very comfortable with their "gut-level feelings." When you feel that "I think I've got it" sense of elation, keep going, trust yourself. If you are thinking in an area where you are knowledgeable, you are more likely to end up right than wrong. This is the creative way.

Criteria. Criteria by which we determine which ideas are best are conscious standards or yardsticks by which we measure the value of our ideas. They introduce a conscious, systematic, deliberate element which helps to organize and focus our conscious and unconscious selection capabilities.

Objectives which are specified for the solution to a particular problem become the criteria by which the best solution is selected. If we are trying to design a better mouse trap, our objective would be to design one which is economical to produce, easy to use, easy to repair, aesthetic and simple. These design objectives are the criteria which help us choose between the various design alternatives.

Different types of problems utilize different criteria. Criteria often used in the measuring of the worth of invention ideas include: costs to manufacture, cost to develop, costs to maintain, simplicity and beauty of the design. Criteria which might be used as an aid to selecting solutions to personal everyday problems often include expenditures required, ease of accomplishments, negative and positive effects on others, amount of effort involved, chance of success and possible result if failure occurs.

Different people choose solutions according to different criteria. A child may choose a piece of candy because of its bright color, whereas an adult may choose it because of its pleasing flavor. One person might choose a vacation location because it is exciting and in the hub of human activity. Others might choose a vacation location because it is remote, tranquil and in the mountains away from other people.

Criteria aren't the only basis for choosing the best idea. They help us choose ideas by aiding our conscious and unconscious minds. It is like the man who carefully listed the criteria by which he planned to select a new car. He wanted it to be attractive, economical, compact, comfortable, contain ample luggage space and have a high resale value. After searching for several days, he found a car that met his criteria very well but he <u>didn't</u> <u>like</u> <u>it</u>. He instead chose an expensive sports car because he "felt like it." Often our conscious criteria reflect what we "think we want" or what we think others think we should want, instead of what we really want, based on our down deep "gut-level feeling" (see Illustration 26). This doesn't mean that we ignore criteria because often times, even if we really want a sports car, we can only truly afford an economical compact.

Thinking vs Feeling
Illustration 26

Idea Selection. After we have reviewed our criteria to help focus
and organize our conscious and unconscious minds, Mind Integrating is a
catalyst which emphasizes the need to trust our "gut-level feelings."
To select the best idea, we review the criteria which we have established
to help evaluate the possible solution ideas to our problem. Then we
eliminate ideas which we "feel" are nonsensical or ridiculous and group
similar ideas. Now we are ready to let our intuition tell us which idea
is the best idea. The use of an idea rating system is discussed later
in this chapter for a more thorough, in-depth approach to selecting the
best idea.

Consider the problem of, "In what ways can we gain more friends?"
Some possible solutions include: join a club, ask people over for dinner, dress nicer, develop a hobby, ask a lot of people to be your friend,
give lots of parties, take people out to dinner, be active in charity
groups, develop a better personality, compliment people, show an interest
in other people, get involved in a group sport, ask your existing friends
to introduce you to new people, become famous, develop better manners,
take a college course, go on a ship cruise, advertise for friends in the
newspaper, move your residence every few years to meet new people and be
helpful to other people. This list is not all inclusive, but is a creative list because it does represent a large number and diversity of ideas
out of which you may find good ideas.

To select the best idea, the possibilities which I "feel" are nonsensical, ridiculous, or too difficult to achieve are eliminated includ--
ing: ask people to be your friend, marry someone with a lot of friends,
develop a better personality, become famous, advertise for friends in the
newspaper and move your residence every few years. Next, similar ideas
are grouped. Ideas which related to joining include: join a club, be
active in a charity group, get involved in a group sport, take a college
course and go on a ship cruise. Ideas which relate to changing oneself
include: Dress nicer, develop a hobby, compliment other people, show an
interest in other people, develop better manners and be helpful to others.
The third grouping includes those ideas which relate to actively and somewhat directly seeking friends: ask people over for dinner, give lots of
parties, take people out to dinner and ask your existing friends to introduce you to new people. All of these ideas offer a possible solution to
the problem depending on our unique personality, goals and needs. However,

-174-

we are trying to select the best solution - the one which we wish to try first.

Criteria which I might use to aid me in the final selection process include: the friends gained should lead to long term in-depth relationships, the effort required to gain friends should be low cost and minimal, and the potential friend should be unaware that I am looking for a friend. After reviewing these criteria, I feel that the best solution for me at this time is to invite people over for dinner. Your choice might be different.

Idea rating can be used to provide a more thorough, in-depth selection of the best idea from the final list of ideas which you have screened and grouped. Idea rating is accomplished by first rating each idea in terms of each criterion; then the ratings for each idea are totaled to help provide further conscious insight prior to the final "gut-level" selection. A scale rated on the basis of 1 for good, 2 for average and 3 for poor would be used. A grid with the ideas listed in rows and the criteria rating in columns can be helpful to this rating process.

The problem solutions discussed earlier for the problem on how to gain more friends is evaluated using idea ratings below. First, the best three or four solutions were selected: invite people over for dinner, join a sports club and dress nicer. Then, each solution idea was rated on a scale of one to three for each criterion. As can be seen in the following example, the solution "dress nicer" was rated 2, average, for the criterion "long-term relationships."

Solutions	Criteria Long-Term Relationships	Low Cost, Minimal Effort	Potential Friend Unaware	Total Rating
1) Invite people over for dinner.	2	2	3	7
2) Join a sports club.	1	3	1	5
3) Dress nicer.	2	3	1	6

1 - for good.
2 - for average.
3 - poor.

The conclusion, according to the total rating approach to selection, is that I should join a sports club. The idea rating system does not guarantee that the best idea receives the lowest rating. You may still feel that inviting others for dinner is the best solution. Trust your feelings. Try that idea first because it is more likely to be correct.

Summary

The Mind Integrating process recognizes that each of us is unique, that our gut-level feelings are based on our unconscious reservoir of knowledge and experience. It utilizes criteria to measure value as a way to focus and organize the conscious and unconscious mental processes in the direction of selecting the best ideas by reviewing them or using a rating grid. The final selection is based on listening to the inner ear, and by trusting our own "gut-level feelings."

Creativity Grows With Exercise!

1. List at least five criteria which you might use to help choose the best idea for the following problems:

   a. What is the best career for me?

   b. Who should be elected president of the U.S.?

   c. Design a better pencil sharpener.

   d. In what ways can I improve my English grammar or written communications?

2. What criteria might the following people use to help select a new car for themselves?

   a. An artist.

   b. An engineer.

   c. A geologist.

   d. A teenager.

   e. An octogenarian.

3. What combination of experiences, knowledge and psychological makeup make you unique as a creative person?

4. Discuss the statement "Objective evaluations are impossible."

5. List at least three criteria which you might use to help choose the best idea from the ideas you developed for those problems listed in problem 1.

6. Develop at least three idea solutions for the following problems. List several criteria to help in the selection process. Use your "gut-level" feelings to select the best three or four ideas. Then use an idea-rating grid to select the final best single idea.

   a. What is creativity?

   b. What driving habit should be developed by drivers to help reduce collisions?

c. What are the most essential ingredients of a happy marriage?

d. How can old tennis balls be used?

e. Design a better frying pan.

f. In what way can companies help develop their employees to their fullest potential?

Strengthen Your Idea   (Mind Strengthen)

Whenever any new idea is presented, there are always those quick to view it with alarm and to "seriously question" its possible strengths and to point out its drawbacks. Criticism should not be completely eliminated, for those expressing such pessimistic negativism must be answered. They provide a balance to the overly optimistic.

The person who originated the idea tends to defend and protest both _valid_ and _invalid_ criticism. It is like a person who, once having decided to marry a particular person, refuses to listen to _any_ criticism of the choice. The result is often an unwise marriage or a marriage which begins with unnecessary weakness due to the half-open eyes of the marriage partners. Leibnitz observed, "I would walk twenty miles to listen to my worst enemy if I could learn something."

Don't pluck failure out of the jaws of success by avoiding the possible strengthening aspects of criticism. Talk to your enemies. Learn from their arguments.

The Mind Strengthening catalyst is designed to help strengthen our mind against our own tendency to avoid self-criticism and criticism from other people. To Mind Strengthen we first clearly identify the negative drawbacks of our ideas, then try to transform the negative drawbacks into positive strengths before others even identify them as drawbacks. This process in effect turns your lemons into lemonade and steals the thunder

-178-

from your critics. As a final step in Mind Strengthening, we modify our idea to satisfy valid criticisms and thereby strengthen our idea. We accentuate the positives and modify the negatives.

Efforts to positivize (make positive) the negative aspects of ideas are very often productive. An airplane wing walker was asked by a reporter about how he was able to overcome his worst enemy, the wind, that he encountered while on the wing. The wing walker's response was that he made the wind work for him. He positioned himself in such a fashion that the wind's force helped hold him on the plane's wing rather than blow him off. He turned his lemon (the wind) into lemonade.

Politicians can often be observed strengthening their position by positivizing their negative aspects. Politicians with publicly known crooked backgrounds often present this crooked background as evidence that they have been through the worst and now know better than to be crooked again. Whereas they portray their honest opponent as a lamb, inexperienced in the "ways of the world" and susceptible to corruption.

If we decide to plant a shade tree near our home, critics could point out that the leaves from the tree will drop all over the roof and lawn, the tree will require constant trimming, it will block the view of the house and it will cause the inside of the house to be darker. To Mind Strengthen, we would first try to positivize these criticisms; the dropping leaves would help us experience the seasons of nature, constant trimming would provide us with good outdoor exercise, blocking the view of the house would provide greater privacy and darkening the inside of the house would keep it cool.

If these attempts at positivizing the negatives don't satisfy us, we could reduce the criticisms and thereby strengthen the idea as follows:

To eliminate the falling leaves, we could plant an evergreen tree. To reduce the required trimming, we could plant a slow-growing tree. To keep the view of the house from being blocked, we could plant the tree near the corner of the house. To keep the inside of the house lighter, we could plant a tree with sparse foliage or plant the tree away from the windows.

I like sayings like, "If you can't be thankful for what you've got... be thankful for what you haven't got." This type of positive thinking may have beneficial results. However, the benefits are often short-lived. If we are stuck with a bad situation such as a broken leg or flat tire, positive thinking can help keep us optimistic and reduce the mental burden of our plight. Like an old Chinese proverb says, "Optimism: A cheerful frame of mind that enables a tea kettle to sing though in hot water up to its nose." However, if positive thinking keeps us from changing a bad situation, positive thinking becomes our enemy. If we are poor or out of shape, positive thinking can prevent growth by allowing us to accept conditions which we could improve.

Mind Strengthening is not "positive thinking." We don't try to replace criticism by assertions like, "My tree won't drop many leaves," or "I will learn to like tree trimming." We are trying to see ideas as they really are, including their strengths and their weaknesses.

Just because a criticism exists, we don't need to immediately give in and modify our idea. We first try to see the positive aspects of the criticism. Perhaps we do savor falling leaves as a sign of the changing seasons. On the other hand, if we don't, we should "see it like it is" and modify our idea. We could plant an evergreen tree in this case, to make our idea stronger. The format which follows provides a systematic framework for the application of the Mind Strengthen creative catalyst.

Idea: Plant a shade tree near our home.

Negative Aspects	Positivized Negatives	Potential Idea Modifications
Leaves will drop on the roof and the lawn.	Falling leaves stimulate an appreciation of nature's seasons.	Plant an evergreen tree.
It will require constant trimming.	Trimming helps obtain outdoor exercise.	Plant a slow-growing tree to reduce trimming needs.
It will block the view of the house.	This gives us greater privacy.	Plant the tree near the corner of the house.
It will cause the inside of the house to be darker.	This will help keep the house cool in the summer.	Plant tree which has sparse foliage away from windows.

Don't think that you have a great idea just because it possesses some positive attributes. As one popular song exclaims, "everything is beautiful in its own way." Don't be complacent with your idea and wait to see if others criticize it. For a moment be your own best critic, look for weak points and faults in your idea, tear it apart. This "clears the way" for positivizing these negative points and modifies your idea to make it even stronger.

Consider the design of a styrofoam coffee cup. The designers could purposely attack their own design as being unattractive, having no handle, being too light, too easy to tip over and not lasting very long. However, before they consider modifying the design they should try to defend the design by positivizing these apparently negative aspects.

The cup is not unattractive but simple and white, which allows it to fit into many coffee-serving environments. It doesn't need a handle because it is well insulated. The lack of a handle reduces the costs

-181-

and adds to the aesthetic simplicity of the design. Its lightness makes people handle the container more carefully and allows for ease in shipping and handling while empty. The fact that the cups are not long lasting is inherent in their low cost and leads to greater number of sales, and therefore greater quantities produced, and therefore again lower costs. The coffee cup designers may reasonably conclude that no design change is necessary.

To use the Mind Strengthening catalyst, attack your own ideas. See your idea from the wealth of experiences and knowledge of others. Psychologists have often used role playing as a method of "seeing" through other's eyes. To role play, you act out the role of another person.

If you are designing a new tennis racquet you might, instead of just asking a tennis player to criticize your design, try to pretend (play the role) that you are a professional tennis player. What would you, playing the role of a professional tennis player, like or dislike about the racquet design? If you are considering trying to gain new friends by inviting people over for dinner, you might imagine (play the role) that you are the person being invited over for dinner and try to experience the reaction to your potential invitation. If you are asking for a pay raise, you might assume the role of your own boss to see how he would respond to your request before you make it.

It is much safer and stronger to know that a person has his doubts, as you and I have ours, yet has the courage to move ahead in spite of these doubts. In contrast to the person who has barricaded himself against valid criticism, the person with the courage to believe in his idea, and at the same time admit and face his doubts, is flexible and open to new possibilities, creative and has a greater chance of success.

Once a solution becomes apparent, there is often a mad rush to put it into practice "as is." Mother complexes engulf us and pet ideas are implemented without a rational preliminary evaluation being performed. However, the solution may be only partially complete, too costly or too complex. Mind Strengthening is a catalyst designed to counter the natural inclination to immediately implement "half baked ideas." It alerts you to the strengths (positive aspects) and weaknesses (negative aspects) of your idea and provides you with a tool to better understand and perhaps modify your idea to make it stronger. Mind Strengthening strengthens you as well as your idea. You gain greater confidence that your idea will survive in the real world.

Creativity Grows With Exercise!

1. List at least three reasons why people may have considered travel by automobile impractical in 1900.

2. List as many reasons as you can why people may have thought bubble gum would never sell well.

3. Discuss the following statements.

   a. "He that wrestles with us strengthens our nerves and sharpens our skill. Our antagonist is our helper."   Edmund Burke

   b. Positive thinking can lead to negative oversights.

   c. "Mishaps are like knives, that either serve us or cut us, as we grasp them by the blade or the handle."   James Russell Lowell

   d. Perfectionistic tendencies in many people may result in ideas never being acted upon (implemented).

4. If your idea is to ask for a raise from your boss, what might his reaction be? Play the role of the boss (imagine that you are the boss). List at least three positive and negative reactions you

might have as the boss to your proposal for a raise.

5. Consider the standard yellow, wood, lead-cored pencil with an eraser on the end. Assume the role of the following people and list their potential positive and negative reactions to the design of a pencil.

   a. A young child.

   b. A retired person.

   c. An engineer.

   d. A teacher.

   e. A manufacturer.

   f. A salesman.

   g. A rich person.

   h. A poor person.

6. Discuss the following statements:

   a. "Please all, and you will please none."   Aesop

   b. "Have you not learned great lessons from those who reject you, and brace themselves against you? or treat you with contempt, or dispute the passage with you?"   Walt Whitman

   c. What is the difference between "positive thinking" and Mind Strengthening?

7. Mind Strengthen the idea that summer vacations are good for elementary school students.

Negative Aspects	Positivized Negative	Idea Modification
Example:		
1. Wastes school facilities.	Stimulates better use the rest of the year.	Use summers to teach subjects of special interest. Also let other nonprofit organizations use facilities during the summer.
Example:		
2. Leaves students bored during the summer.	Makes them more excited to return to school.	Provide summer school for those students who desire it.
3.		
4.		
5.		

8. Use the Mind Strengthening catalyst and format shown in problem 7 on the following ideas.

   a. People should all work from 8 a.m. to 5 p.m., five days a week.

   b. The standard desk stapler.

   c. A standard wood toothpick.

   d. Automobiles should be eliminated from our transportation system.

   e. Household garbage should be recycled.

   f. The creativity of everyone should be developed.

   g. No one's creativity should be developed.

Energize Yourself to Act (Mind Energize)

"Doubts are traitors," wrote Shakespeare, "and make us lose the good we oft might win by fearing to attempt." Often we have a good idea or solution to a problem which dies because we don't have the courage and energy to transform it into action. Worse yet, we may let it linger in our mind, resulting in a foggy, muddled mind. Mind Energizing is a technique for increasing our capacity to exert the energy required to actualize our ideas or to clear our mind by rejecting our ideas as being too risky to implement or not worthy of our time and effort. Basically, at this point in the problem-solving process, a "go" or "no go" decision is necessary. Mind Energizing helps us to be decisive and thereby exert our maximum effort to follow our idea through to its greatest possible potential, or to drop it now.

In most sports, the value of following through is drilled into the athletes. For example, in golf and tennis, following through on your stroke is essential to being a good golfer or tennis player. It takes practice, energy and decisiveness to follow through. Mind Energizing helps develop the capacity to follow the implementation of our ideas through to success, and makes us more effective creative thinkers.

During the idea selection phase of problem solving, advantages and disadvantages of the various ideas have been compared, and one idea has been selected for implementation. The central approach to Mind Energize is to exaggerate the best and worst possible consequences of implementing an idea and then, if necessary, modify the idea to minimize its worst consequences and maximize its best consequences. In effect, Mind Energize helps us examine and modify our idea so that it has the greatest chance of success.

In the area of nuclear energy, the best result of widespread use of nuclear reactors to generate electricity might be low-cost power. The worst possible result might be a nuclear excursion (loss of control of a nuclear reactor) at a power plant. A nuclear power plant excursion is dangerous (a bad consequence) enough to warrant a design requirement being imposed on nuclear power plants called the maximum credible accident. The maximum credible accident examines the worst imaginable possible combination of causes. For example, one coastal power plant is designed to be able to sustain a substantial tidal wave, even though the probability of one occurring is very small. Once the worst consequence is minimized, nuclear power developments are able to move forward in a more confident, energetic fashion with the implementation of this low-cost form of energy.

Professional tennis player, Timothy Gallwey, presents an example of what I have labeled Mind Energizing in his book The Inner Game of Tennis. After completing one match in a tennis tournament, Gallwey wrote:

"I began thinking immediately of my next match against a highly ranked player in northern California. I knew that he was a more experienced tournament player than I and probably more skilled. I certainly didn't want to play the way I had during the first round; it would be a rout. But my knees were still shaky, my mind didn't seem able to focus clearly, and I was nervous. Finally, I sat down in seclusion to see if I could come to grips with myself. I began asking myself, 'What's the worst that can happen?' The answer was easy; 'I could lose 6-0, 6-0.' 'Well, what if you did? What then?' 'Well...I'd be out of the tournament and go back to Meadowbrook. People would ask me how I did, and I would say that I lost in the second round to So-and-So.' They'd say sympathetically, 'Oh, he's pretty tough. What was the score?' Then I would have to confess; love and love. 'What would happen next?' I asked myself. 'Well, word would quickly get around that I had been trounced up at Berkeley, but soon I'd start playing well again and before long life would be back to normal.'

"I had tried to be as honest as I could about the worst possible results. They weren't good, but neither were they unbearable--certainly not bad enough to get upset about. Then I asked myself, 'What's the best that could happen?' Again the answer was clear; I could win 6-0, 6-0. 'Then what?'"

The positive consequences of playing the second match were much more energizing than the negative consequences. This apparently relaxed him and provided him with the energy necessary to play a better game of tennis than he would have played otherwise.

If you are considering asking for a raise, you could Mind Energize by comparing the worst that could happen if you ask for the raise with the best that could happen. The worst that could happen, depending on your boss, would be that you would not get the raise and your boss would think less of you for having asked. The best that could happen is that you would get the raise, the boss would become pleased with your self-assertive behavior and you would be able to obtain even higher wages later.

If this analysis does not energize you to ask for the raise, try to modify your request for a raise to minimize the potential negative consequence. Perhaps, instead of bluntly asking for a raise, you could tactfully help your boss become aware that you are dissatisfied with your present wage or that other people doing similar work are getting paid more. Then you must decide to "do it" and ask for the raise or forget it and focus your mind and energies on something else.

Vitality tends to stem from being active. One of the realities of life is that energy expended by a person tends to create additional energy. So energize yourself. Decide to implement your ideas now, or clear the air for doing something else. The worst possible consequence of most problem solving efforts is that you do nothing. That is, you don't decide to implement your idea, to drop it and move on to something else.

A format for the Mind Energize process follows:

1. List worst and best consequences of implementing the idea.

2. Modify the idea to minimize the worst consequence and maximize the best consequence.

3. Decide whether or not to use your energy to implement the idea.

If you are careful enough and never try to implement anything, nothing good or bad will ever happen to you! On the other hand, remember that the apparently smart man often uses his energy to get out of predicaments that an effective creative thinker wouldn't have gotten into in the first place. Don't be like many people who spend their lives minimizing losses rather than maximizing gains. Use Mind Energize to help provide you with enough energy to do something worthwhile with your creative ideas.

Creativity Grows With Exercise!

1. Present at least one good and one bad consequence which might occur in the future if the following prophecy ideas for the year 2000 were actualized. Then suggest a way, or ways, to modify the idea such that the bad consequences are minimized and the good consequences are maximized.

a. Everyone will have the right to have a private garden plot.

b. Living quarters will be flexible enough to allow easy rearrangements daily.

c. Very cheap electrical power will be made available.

d. Poverty will be eliminated.

e. Every family will own three cars.

f. Artists will be supported by public grants.

2. List three prophecies of your own. Strengthen them by listing their good and bad potential consequences. Then suggest a way or ways to modify the ideas such that the bad consequences are minimized and the good consequences are maximized.

3. Apply Mind Energize to decide whether or not to transform into action the following ideas:

   a. Smokeless ashtray.

   b. Book on capital punishment.

   c. Pencil lead eraser as big as a chalk eraser.

   d. Helicopter service between San Franciso and Oakland (San Francisco and Oakland about 20 miles apart; the San Francisco Bay separates them).

4. Name several magazines which utilize the essence of this process to present information; for example, Consumer Reports.

Chapter 10

TRANSFORM IDEAS INTO ACTION
(Creative ideas are not enough!)

"Action without intelligence is a form of insanity, but intelligence
without action is the greatest form of stupidity in the world," observed
inventor Charles F. Kettering. The creative process does not end with
a good solution to a problem--it begins with one. The solution to a
problem presents a creative challenge which usually requires the maximum
use of our creativity. As Professor John Arnold of Stanford University
observed:

> "Few ideas are in themselves practical. It is for the want of
> active imagination in their application, rather than in their
> means of acquisition, that they fail. The creative process does
> not end with an idea--it only starts with an idea."

Edison wrote, "Genius is one percent inspiration and 99% perspira-
tion." We often have inspirational ideas, but for most of us our
creative genius is lost because our creative ideas fail like leaves
around us and rot. Perhaps we don't recognize that creativity is one
percent thinking it, and ninety-nine percent doing it.

The president of Inventors Workshop International, Melvin L. Fuller,
stated that getting a good idea for an invention is as easy as getting
pregnant. Perhaps we might consider implementing an idea as being as
difficult as it is to properly raise a child once it has been born.
Many research studies have shown that, at least below the genius level
of intelligence, success depends less on the ability to think of something and more on the ability to do something with our thoughts - -

transforming them into action.

Implementation of an average idea is far superior to thinking of an outstanding idea. Often times we become perpetual thinkers about ideas and their possibilities with the delusion that some day we will have the perfect idea and will then be willing to do something with it. Storing up ideas in the mental barn forever is a good way to avoid action and keep the barn from other more useful purposes.

The DO IT acronym is used as a call to action. Too often when we think about doing it, we somehow feel that we are as successful as those who do DO IT. We often hear statements like, "I could have bought IBM stock at $30 a share. If I had, I would be rich now," or "I thought about the idea for a particular new invention years before it came on the market," or "If I would have applied myself, I could have become a basketball star." We have all probably had thoughts like these. Often we feel that having had the thought makes us almost as successful as those who transformed their thoughts into action (see Illustration 27). Not true! Success is not ninety-nine percent thinking and one percent action. Directed, applied, creative action dominates the successful person's life.

Thinking vs Doing
Illustration 27

If one person tells you about an idea he has for a great book but does not write the book, and another has the same idea and does write it, the second person might be called creative. But we couldn't say the same about the first. He is a creative talker, not a creative writer.

Few things can put the brake on creativity like waiting for the breaks. Many of us go through life like the tourists walking through Hollywood waiting for a limousine to pull up, a producer step out, tap them on the shoulder and say, "I want to make you a movie star."

Many times the people who become the stars or get to the top are not the ones with the greatest ideas or potential, but the ones who do something with their ideas and potentials. They try their ideas. They actively seek uses of their potentialities. The unsuccessful person is an observer of action, rather than one who takes action and tries to do something. The most trying person of all is the one who doesn't try.

Anyone who has worked in an organizational environment knows only too well that it is hard enough to get anything done, let alone to do something creative or innovative. A great new idea can hang around a company for years and not be implemented because no one has taken the initiative to transform the words and thought into action. Creative action is often more important to a company than creative ideas.

Once we have an idea, we need to descend from the clouds and put it to work. We need to transform it into action. The seed becomes a flower, the puppy a dog and the pollywog a frog naturally. For a person to deliberately transform an idea into action requires day-to-day courage, commitment, persistence and flexibility. It requires a truly creative effort.

A Marine officer once said that one of the sayings of the Marines is "do something--even if it is wrong!" If you are trapped in a foxhole-- do something--attack, retreat or dig deeper. Don't just sit there waiting for fate to run its course. When you have an idea, do something, even if it's wrong. Give up the idea and clear your mind of it if you don't think it is good. Otherwise, begin the process of transforming it into action.

Persistence

It took Columbus fourteen years to sell his proposed voyage. The Xerox copying process was available four years before a financial backer could be found. When Bell first offered his telephone for sale, it was turned down because "there was no need for it." Crude preparations of penicillin were described in 1929, but nobody followed through on the

-194-

discovery for many years. Persistence, resolutely proceeding in spite of opposition, was necessary to transform these ideas into action.

When the flying shuttle was invented by John Kay, it was considered to be such a threat to labor that weavers mobbed him and destroyed the mold for his shuttle. In 1844, Horace Wells was the first doctor to use gas on patients while pulling teeth. The medical profession scorned his idea as humbug. As Thomas Edison observed, "Society is never prepared to receive any invention. Every new thing is resisted and it takes years for the inventor to get people to listen to him and years more before it can be introduced."

"In science the credit goes to the man who convinces the world, not to the man to whom the idea first occurs," observed Sir William Osler. Many people other than Columbus, Kay, Bell, Wells and Edison have had great ideas. In fact most of us have had great ideas but the credit goes to those who transform their ideas into action.

To transform ideas into action, we must overcome the obstacles which other people present, overcome the obstacles we impose on ourselves, maintain a positive attitude, be willing to modify our solution and follow the idea through to completion.

Emerson considered thought to be the seed of action. To transform an idea seed into action takes a resolute commitment to follow the idea through to completion. Perhaps Christ's remark that "the spirit is strong but the flesh is weak," relates to the problem we have as creative people: We are very excited by our new idea, but easily discouraged when we face the work required to make the idea work, overcome the resistance of others and finally transform it into action.

<u>Resistance From Others</u>. Many of us pride ourselves on having an open mind. More often than not, an open mind means that we stick to our opinions and let others have theirs. This provides us with a pleasant sense of tolerance and apparent lack of bias. True open-mindedness is more than this. It is a mind open to considering the ideas of other people as possibly valid and distrusting our own initial ideas.

Picasso once remarked that,"Every act of creation is first of all an act of destruction." A new idea often destroys what a lot of us believe to be essential to survival and order in the world. The newer the idea, and the greater the importance of the idea, the greater is the destruction and subsequent anxiety it causes in us. We tend to resist ideas in proportion to how new they are, how great an impact they may have on us, and how much they depart from habit and tradition.

Don't rock the boat--things are going well just as they are! Fear of loss, not profit, often dominates business and personal decision making. This is the prime reason inventors experience such great difficulty in gaining the backing of businessmen or financing for the actualization of their ideas.

Businessmen are not generally interested in ideas. They are interested in established products. Once you have developed a company to manufacture your idea and sales are proceeding well, the business world believes your idea is the "real thing." Then they are ready to buy your idea. Even Edison had to use this approach to sell some of his own patents. He had forty-five patents on reading and optical character recognition machines. He couldn't sell them, so he opened a business using the patents and ten years later sold the company to a major corporation.

Inventors and other creative people often lack the appearances, social graces and salesmanship expected by others. Society often judges people on the basis of appearances. If the cover isn't pretty, the book is no good. However, creative people often believe that their idea is so excellent that it doesn't need to be sold, and that selling or promoting their own idea is unprofessional and beneath their dignity. Therefore, their ideas often fail because of the way they are presented, not because they are unsound ideas.

I know a successful engineer with a master's degree from the California Institute of Technology who developed a transportation plan which would produce phenomenal results--greatly reduce the consumption of energy, emission of pollutants and increase safety. When I met him, he had been trying to interest governmental, industrial and educational institutions in funding his idea. In spite of his professional experience and the worthiness of his idea, he found it difficult to get others to read his brief summary report, to answer his letter or to talk to him about it for even a few minutes. He found that even his best friends would not readily read his brief report on his idea.

People are so involved in meeting their own day-to-day needs and following established patterns that the first task of a person with an idea is simply to get their attention; get them to listen to the proposal. Even advertisers of established products use gimmicks such as pretty girls, catch songs and silly or even apparently stupid advertisement to bring attention to their product.

During my first year as an Assistant Professor at a large university, I attended a large student-faculty meeting which was called to air problems related to instruction at the University. During the course of the discussion, I decided to reveal that I felt a large percentage of the faculty in my department were incompetent as teachers. My hands were clammy and my voice shook with nervousness when I spoke.

I expected a stormy discussion to ensue after I made my comments. To my surprise and disappointment, no one even responded to my remarks. The interest and attention of the participants shifted immediately to the next person who came to the platform. In retrospect, I see that, as often occurs, the participants were so wrapped up in what they planned to say, in their ideas and points of view, that they barely heard mine. I didn't even get their attention.

People make decisions. Good salesmanship recognizes that we need to sell ourselves and our ideas to people. We need to give them choices, demonstrate practicality, use the testimony of others, emphasize mutual interest, draw favorable comparisons and present the unique advantages of our ideas.

Let the other person have your way. Convince him that your way and his way are one in the same. Don't do it if it isn't true. However, if you do have a good idea, and are selling it to the right person, it is usually beneficial to both of you that it be transformed into action. The term salesman has a bad connotation because it often represents the sale of an item to someone who doesn't want it or can't afford it. Be genuine. Have warm regard for others. It will pay off in the long run.

We are all in a sense competing for the attention of others. They are consciously or unconsciously asking, "Why should I give you some of my precious time?" "What can you do for me?" and "Who are you?" Even when we get their attention, we must recognize that they are uniquely different people with distinct interests, personalities and objectives. We may come to our boss feeling good about a clever idea for improving working conditions. However, he may be much more interested in how much it costs to implement or whether it increases employee productiveness rather than in the cleverness of our idea.

Often the personal appearance, attributes and the level of achievement of others are used as conscious or unconscious excuses or mechanisms for restricting the amount of new ideas we allow ourselves to consider. We say to ourselves: He couldn't have a good idea, he's only been with the company for six months; women always have silly ideas; uneducated people are just shooting in the dark for ideas; a loud-mouth like her couldn't possibly have a good idea; a report with poor spelling, grammar or punctuation can't possibly be valid; it is a fact that if you have an M.D. degree instead of no degree and offer a new idea on child care, more people will pay attention to you; if you are the president of a company, others will listen to you more carefully.

This is a form of discrimination. We all use it to survive the great number of new ideas and thoughts which bombard us. This is the way life is! It's part of everyone's nature! Recognize it and persist accordingly! Recognize that you must present yourself and your idea well to even get the valuable attention of other people. Try to enlist the support of experts in the field, or other prominent "listened to" people, to help you promote your idea and bring it into the limelight.

Resistance From Self. Any creative effort will always develop resistance and discouragement in others and some amount of self-discouragement, uncertainty and fear of failure in ourselves. This is often the biggest barrier which exists to the successful implementation of our own creative ideas.

Often we blame our self-discouragement on an unresponsive public, uncreative environment, narrow-minded boss, simple-minded businessman or lack of financial resources. These factors are real and do provide seed for discouragement! However, the fact is that all creative people face these same obstacles, but the successful ones persist in spite of them.

To do something with a creative idea, we must risk losing an idea by exposing it to others. If we send a script for a play to a producer or outline for a book to a publisher, they may "steal" it. When we reveal a possibly patentable idea to an attorney, he may "steal" it. When we tell our boss about an idea for saving the company money, he may "steal" it.

A patent attorney told me that some people have entered his office with things in a paper bag behind their back, asking for advice but refusing to reveal their idea for fear it might be stolen (see illustration 28). The fear is real. People do steal ideas. But, if we don't trust someone to some extent, we cannot transform them into action. Determine the reputation of the patent attorney, have copies of your notes, outlines or ideas dated and witnessed by others before revealing them to the attorney, but don't become discouraged and give up at that point simply because someone might steal your idea.

Many times we stop cold in our path toward implementation because we don't want to share the acclaim or financial benefits with others. No one is going to finance your invention or play your music without a substantial share of the profits and often the acclaim. Bosses usually do share the acclaim due to the ideas of their employees. Rightly or wrongly, our society perceives the leader (boss) to be a significant factor in the creativity of his employees. If you refuse to share the benefits of your ideas with others, even those you feel don't deserve it, you may lose all the potential benefits because it may never be implemented.

Trust?

Illustration 28

The prominent psychologist, Abraham H. Maslow, when undertaking a new project, indicated he encountered many big talkers, great planners and tremendously enthusiastic people who wanted to help him. He was interested to see if these people were willing to work hard, and tested them by giving them a rather dull but important and worthwhile job to do. Nineteen out of twenty failed the test.

Often actors, inventors or artists are acclaimed as "overnight" successes. People forget the years of failure, small triumphs and just dogged persistence which are the dues paid by almost all successful people. Most of us aren't aware of, and don't have the time or resources required to persist in the transformation of an idea into action. However, it has been my observation that most of the time we give up before we need to, or before we should--we get tired and discouraged. This is natural. However, the successfully creative people don't give up forever. They may walk away from their work for a few minutes, hours, days, months or even years, but eventually, if they believe in their idea, they persist and work their way to completion.

Hemingway remarked that when a solution comes alive, you better be ready to fight it through to the bloody end. Often we give up before the fight begins. We aren't willing to exert the energy and effort required to fight it through and face the failures and bloody blows along the way.

Frustration and anxiety are inherent to the creative process; will the idea really work, will people ever stop "knocking it," will I have the energy to follow it through, what are others saying about me? The creative person recognizes the eventuality of frustration and anxiety, but, as the psychologist Rollo May observed, the creative person has the courage to follow his idea through to completion.

The persistence of creative people, in spite of the self-imposed and environmentally-imposed obstacles, can be attributed to their attitude about the process and their self concept. Confucius commented that "Habits take us where we were yesterday and our attitudes keep us there." Poor attitudes support existing habits and accept the eventuality of obstacles and roadblocks.

As William James observed, "Human beings can alter their lives by altering their attitudes." If we have an attitude that we can succeed, that obstacles can be overcome, we can persist. Abraham Lincoln commented, "Always bear in mind that your own resolution to succeed is more important than any other one thing." The difference between successful creative people and many of us is not the differences in problems, but differences in our attitudes toward problems.

Modification

Large industrial companies have research and development divisions. The research basically generates the idea. The development effort transforms the idea by a process of testing it and modifying it into a usable reality.

Most of our ideas begin as soft insights which modification and development harden into the hard finished steel of creation. Once the idea has been formulated, it must be patched, modified and simplified to help it grow to completion. The idea must be prepared for the specific purpose for which it is to be used to prevent possible snags in its transformation into action. Perhaps it has to be made more reliable, aesthetic, longer lasting, easier to repair, safer or more efficient. Maybe it is too costly, hard to produce, sell or maintain.

Our efforts to transform an idea into action will succeed only if our persistence includes a large number of fluid, flexible idea modifications. Creative people are not only fluid and flexible in producing ideas, they are also fluid and flexible in the transformation of their ideas into action.

When do we abandon one strategy or one aspect of an idea for another? When is rigid perseverance a virtue and flexibility a curse? Too much perseverance is considered to represent stubbornness. Too much flexibility is considered to represent a wishy-washy attitude. We must be fully committed to our original idea and at the same time aware that we might be wrong. As the philosopher Voltaire observed, "Doubt is uncomfortable, but certainty is ridiculous."

The proper balance of flexibility and perseverance becomes more evident with experience, like the mechanic who with experience learns the proper amount of torque to apply to a nut--not so little that it may loosen too easily and fall off, and not so much that it will bind and perhaps ruin the threads.

An approach often used to help insure some consideration for possible modification is to leave the idea in a messy, preliminary half-baked form initially. Then, during the process of implementation, to develop it into a firm finished product. Many designers get good results by making their first designs from paper, clay and/or toothpicks. As they play with the initial formulation, they modify and mold it into a finished product. Authors often write a book quickly and sloppily to first get something on paper. Only later do they return to "clean it up" and revise it for publication.

Optimum

Our objective during the transformation-into-action phase of problem solving is to modify our idea to make it more optimum. Our idea should be modified to a condition where it possesses the greatest chance of success. It should not be too complex nor too simple, and not too expensive nor too cheap. It shouldn't be too pretty, nor too plain.

Like fruit we eat, we want our ideas to be modified into an optimum state before we implement them. We don't want to pick fruit too soon nor too late. We want to pick it at an optimum time, when it tastes just right (see illustration 29).

Optimization
Illustration 29

As we modify our idea, we need to seek optimum conditions to enhance its chances of success. Beginners at anything usually have difficulty in achieving optimum conditions. Beginning distance runners
either run races too slow and lose, or run too fast and are not able to
complete the race. Beginning car drivers generally lurch down the road
swaying back and forth until they learn to release the brake and control
the steering at an optimum rate.

Runners, drivers and creative thinkers must find optimum conditions
in the same way. They try the extremes before they eventually achieve
the optimum condition through experience. We as creative thinkers sometimes think too seriously or too relaxed, think for too long or too
short a time, develop ideas which are too radical or too commonplace.
It is through experience, the continual modification of our ideas and
approaches to creative thinking that we become successful creative thinkers and function in a manner which is optimum.

Follow Through

No one is perfect and no idea is perfect. Don't seek perfection.
The modification process could continue forever. There comes a time to

"fish or cut bait." There are always dark days, periods of uncertainty and disillusionment. Go ahead, in spite of difficulties; chances are that this will lead to success.

Sometimes we assume the posture of waiting to do something until life gets easier. The time is now. Take your idea and try it. Thomas Jefferson wrote that, "The ground of liberty must be gained by inches....We are not to be translated from despotism to liberty in a feather bed." Likewise creativity is a game of inches. Our ideas are transformed into acttion in small steps. Don't insist on overnight success. Plan your efforts so that small steps, easier steps lead to conquering the hard overall process.

It takes courage to persist, overcome your and others' resistances, modify your idea and transform it into action. All creative people experience difficulties and anxiety, but they more often than not persist to completion. Forgive yourself for occasionally giving up, not making the best use of your time, being anxious, insecure and nervous about your idea. But don't give up. Come back to it! Fight it through, as Hemingway said, to the bloody end. You will be glad that you did.

Creativity Grows With Exercise!

1. Discuss the following statements.

   a. "Life is not long, and too much of it must not pass in idle deliberation on how it shall be spent."   Samuel Johnson

   b. Do something, even if it is wrong!

   c. The world is never ready for a new idea.

2. Modify the following items into many different terms by making them longer or shorter, combining them into one piece, dividing them into separ smaller parts, making them wide or narrow, square or oval, light or heavy,

fluid or movable, multi-purposed or single-purposed.

a. Table.

b. Pencil.

c. Hat.

d. Chair.

e. Barbecue.

f. Bookshelf.

g. Paperweight.

h. Book.

3. Use Mind Grip, Free and Prompt to solve the following problems:

a. In what ways can we determine if an invention idea needs modification?

b. In what ways do people dodge the action necessary to transform an idea into action?

c. What reaction do people typically have to a new idea?

d. What are honest, genuine approaches to salesmanship?

e. In what ways can we show our genuine warmth for our fellow man?

4. Use any or all of the DO IT catalysts to creative thinking to help generate at least thirty ideas for the following problems.

a. In what ways can we help others do something with their ideas?

b. In what ways can we overcome the resistance of others to our ideas?

c. In what ways can we help ourselves do something with our good ideas?

5. Interview three creative people or leaders to determine the role that persistence plays in their lives.

Planning for Action

"But I've given you the idea--what more do you want?" The central problem that exists once we have a creative idea is what to do with it. This new problem of "How do I transform my idea into action?" requires our best creative problem-solving efforts. The first step of the transformation-into-action process is to "decide when to do what"; that is, develop a plan. As creative people, we should control events with a plan instead of letting them control us.

We have remarked that becoming more creative means that we must, at times during the creative process, be playful and childlike. Yet children live in a world free from significant responsibility and work. They are not blamed for their mistakes. In fact, the law absolves them from responsibility for many of their actions. As creative adults, we must not only originate good ideas, we must assume the responsibility of developing a plan to use as a basis for transforming our ideas into action. We must also follow through on that plan to see that our idea is successfully implemented.

One of Parkinson's Laws is that work expands to fill the available time. If we are given three days to write a difficult letter, we will probably be mentally consumed by the chore for all three days, but actually write the letter in a few hours during the last few hours of the third day.

Most of us have experienced the mad rush of packing the night before a vacation, the last-minute studying for a final exam, or the rush of preparing dinner and cleaning the house just before our dinner guests are about to arrive. As deadlines approach, we shift our energy and focus to the required effort which results in a burst of productivity. Planning actions and deadlines for achieving them helps us keep on the track and focus the energy required to get the job done on time.

A plan helps to set deadlines which allow ample time to achieve the work, but not enough time to be wasteful. A plan is not a slave driver. It is a servant of the creative workers, helping them be more efficient.

If you are in a classroom and are asked, "What would you do if this room suddenly burst into flames?" You might respond, "I am not sure," or, "Let me think about it for a few minutes." On the other hand, if the room did burst into flames, you would do something--ideas would come to you immediately. Deadlines used in planning can't produce the same motivation for doing something as a real fire would, but they can help keep our efforts kindling, progressing toward completion.

The five W's and one H question help provide us with a means of establishing a plan of action. We first ask ourselves, "What should be done?" Then for each "what," we need to answer the question, "Why should it be done?" "Where should it be done?" "Who should do it?" "When should it be done?" and "How should it be done?"

Consider the problem of transforming an invention idea into action. What should be done? Make a working model, obtain a patent, test market it, modify and simplify it, get it into production, sell it and earn a profit.

Why do we need a working model? - ideas are not patentable but working devices are patentable. So we must concentrate our first efforts on making a working model. How should it be done? - using wood instead of steel. Where should it be done? - in my garage. Who should do it? - a skilled craftsman working with me. When should it be done? - by the end of next week.

Why do we need a patent? - to protect the invention from unauthorized use by others. How should it be done? - with the aid of a patent

attorney. Where should it be done? - at the Patent Office by a local attorney. Who should do it? - a patent attorney with a proven record of
honesty and success. When should it be done? - as soon as the working
model is completed, the patent process should begin.

Why do we need to test market it? - because before we invest substantial time, money and effort, we need to see if anyone else is interested in
it enough to purchase it. How should it be done? - a small number of the
inventions should be produced and an effort made to sell them to stores
and/or individuals. Where should it be done? - in areas that might have
a use for our invention. Who should do it? - preferably a person with
proven sales or marketing ability. When should it be done? - as soon as
the patent attorney feels you have a patentable idea and he is far enough
along in the patent process to assure its protection.

These same What, Why, Where, Who, When and How questions should be
asked of every aspect of what needs to be done to transform an idea into
action in a systematic fashion. This type of planning doesn't guarantee
success or eliminate the need for hard work. However, it does help insure
that we work smart as well as hard, effectively as well as efficiently.

Even if we do not want to implement our idea ourselves, we need a
plan to effectively present it to others. Bosses, for example, are bom-
barded with many good ideas. However, few of these ideas are accompanied
by good plans for their implementation and as a result are ignored (see
illustration 30).

Other types of questions which we can use to help us plan our action
include: Are tests required? How much money and time are we willing to
use? Can other people be of help? Is special tooling or skill required?
How can we gain attention and acceptance for the idea? How often should

we reevaluate and update our plan?

The "whens" of a plan can often mean the difference between life and death of an idea. When do we do what? Two important "whens" are when is the best time during the day to work and when should I introduce my idea?

An Idea With a Plan
Illustration 30

Most writers find it easier to work in the morning. Ernest Hemingway remarked: "The earliest part of the morning is the best for me. I awake always at first light and get up and start working." However, some prefer to work in the afternoon or in the middle of the night. John O'Hara observed, "My working time is late at night." Each of us needs to determine when we work best, when we are most alert, productive and effective. Planning a time of day to work not only greatly influences the productivity of your effort, but also affects whether or not you engage in much work at all. If you are working at a poor time of the day, you will probably not enjoy your work and tend to avoid it.

If an idea is ahead of its time, it benefits no one. Also, if it is too late, it is of little use. If we developed a great anti-smog device before there was great concern and legislation to limit pollution, there would be little interest in it. On the other hand, if we developed a new type of engine as good as, or even slightly better than, those presently in use, there would probably be little interest because a solution to that problem already exists.

On a smaller scale, timing may have a dramatic effect. If we ask for a pay raise the day after our company reported a great loss in earnings, or on the day our boss isn't feeling well, we may greatly reduce our chance of success. Many salesmen concentrate their sales calls in industry on Tuesday, Wednesday and Thursday because on Monday customers tend to be getting started and planning their week with little time available for salesmen, whereas on Friday they may be meeting deadlines or tired or grumpy. A good planner must not only plan when to act in terms of how much time is available, but also in terms of when would it be an advantageous time to take the action.

Too much and too rigid planning can be as harmful as no planning. When we plan, we are trying to see the future and, as we all know, anything can happen to the best of plans. As a result, most plans should be general enough to provide room for modification and flexible enough to adjust to the unexpected. They should include the Who, What, Where, Why, When and How of the implementation process.

Creativity Grows With Exercise!

1. Discuss the following statements:

    a. "Perhaps the most valuable result of all education is the abil-
    ity to make yourself do the thing you have to do, when it ought
    to be done, whether you like it or not...however early a man's
    training begins, it is probably the last lesson that he learns
    thoroughly."   Thomas Huxley

    b. Work expands to fill the available time. (One of Parkinson's
    Laws.)

    c. Too much planning can be harmful.

2. What should be done to transform the following ideas into action?
   Be creative, list at least five "whats" for each idea, don't worry
   about quality, then circle the best two "whats."

    a. A new type of razor blade.

    b. A request for a promotion.

    c. Formation of a new toy company.

    d. Going on a diet.

3. Use Mind Prompt and Surprise to help develop at least ten "hows"
   for each "what" idea in problem 2. Use Mind Strengthen to improve
   one of the "hows" for each idea.

4. Develop Whats, Whys, Hows, Where, Whos and Whens for transforming
   the following ideas into action.

    a. A new type of roofing material.

    b. A desire to ask a friend out to dinner.

    c. Building a new patio corner.

    d. A desire to be a better public speaker.

5. When would be the best time of day, day of the week and month of the

year to:

a. Go to the beach.

b. Ask your boss for a promotion.

c. Study for a test.

d. Read.

e. Build a home.

f. Be creative.

Risk and Failure

Our experience in education, business and the professions breeds in us a fear of failure. We must pass all of our tests, make all good business decisions, and make no professional mistakes. In contrast, as Kettering often remarked, an inventor is almost always failing. He tries and fails perhaps a thousand times. If he succeeds once, he has made it. Being creative and transforming ideas into action involves risk and failure.

Robert Louis Stevenson remarked, "Give me the young man who has brains enough to make a fool of himself." It's not failure which blocks creativity. It's giving up when you fail, not recognizing that failure is part of the game or not learning from the failure and proceeding. Implementation of a good idea most often is the reward for those who survive the frustration of many false starts and failures.

"When I was a young man," wrote George Bernard Shaw, "I observed that nine out of ten things I did were failures. I didn't want to be a failure, so I did ten times more work," The road to creative success is littered with failure. Learn to use your failures and mistakes as stepping-stones to success.

One president of Harvard University had a plaque on his wall similar to that in illustration 31 which stated, "Behold the turtle; he makes

progress only when his neck is out." He recognized the need to face
risk and failure as a necessity to growth and progress.

BEHOLD THE TURTLE:
HE MAKES PROGRESS ONLY WHEN HIS NECK IS OUT

Risk Taking
Illustration 31

It is difficult to overestimate the halting effect of fear of failure. Perfectionists are usually not as creative as they could be. Even
the fear of a very small failure inhibits their progress. One medical
researcher found that headaches are most common among perfectionists.
He reported that one out of ten headaches is caused by fear in people
who are afraid of making mistakes.

Most fears of failure are unfounded. We over exaggerate our own
self-importance and the reaction of others to our ideas. The psychologist Abraham Maslow wrote in <u>Eupsychian Management</u>, "I have learned the
novice can often see things that the expert overlooks. All that is necessary is not to be afraid of making mistakes, or of appearing naive."

When all else fails, try trying. Starting over again is creative
too. The secret is to win over adversity. Never stop trying. If you
are knocked down in the process, turn the knockdowns into comebacks (see
Illustration 32).

Trying
Illustration 32

Product Failure. Research indicates that between five and twenty percent of new industrial products have proven profitable. These statistics
include those which are developed within existing companies. Therefore,
if you as an individual are trying to generate, develop, manufacture and
sell a new product on your own, you will probably have even less chance of
achieving success.

Some of the more often cited reasons for the failure include: defects
in the products, poor financing, poor timing, competition reaction, insufficient marketing and higher than anticipated cost. The less you think
systematically and creatively, the greater the chance will be that unforeseen defects will appear in the product, that it will be underfinanced,
that our competition may have or will introduce a similar but better or
cheaper product, that we will flounder in our marketing effort and that
unforeseen events will lead to higher anticipated cost.

Ways to Reduce the Risk of Failure. In business and personal efforts
to grow, to increase our emotional and financial assets and to contribute
to the well-being of our fellow man, we continually face the risks of

failure. We should face these risks realistically and function effectively in spite of them.

Business Growth. A company can deliberately grow in the primary ways; it can extend existing products into new areas of application; it can acquire existing successful products from other companies or it can introduce new products.

The safest approach is to maximize profits by extending existing products into new areas of application. The company knows the existing products well, how to market them, their strengths and weaknesses. A company is likely to experience the fewest surprises and unforeseen risks when it stays with products where it is strong and has the greatest resources.

Acquiring existing successful products from other companies offers the next least risk. These products are proven and the markets are somewhat established. The primary questions which remain include: Can it be purchased at a reasonable price, do the existing resources of the company support a product of this nature and to what degree can sales and profits be increased once the product is acquired?

In general, the most risky approach is to develop new products into new markets. The chance of failure is high but the potential for profit is often extremely high.

Most companies pursue some combination of these and other possibilities. Usually they expend most of their efforts and resources on the safest approach; doing more of the same, introducing nothing new. Depending on their long and short range growth goals, they may introduce new applications of existing products and some new product lines.

Personal Growth. Like business growth, personal growth often depends on the degree of risk we are willing to take; we can rely on "natural" maturation growth and use existing ideas; apply our known resources into new areas; try new ideas which have worked for others, or experiment on our own.

Business growth is extremely complex involving such things as the nature of the finances, personnel, competition and stockholders. Personal growth is even more complex, involving conscious and unconscious needs and goals; physical, emotional and mental resources; financial, job and family environment; and social, legal and theological interactions. However, the same type of strategy can be used as is used by businesses to minimize risks while maximizing growth. Like business, we should use most of our resources for natural habitual growth. This is the safest but slowest approach to growth. Some small amount of our energy should be applied to trying new areas--ideas which have worked for others and new ideas of our own. Many large companies apply as little as one percent of their resources on new ideas and basic research with dramatically positive results. I believe and have experienced that, if you apply one percent of your resources about fifteen minutes a day toward the creative pursuits of originality, you will profit tremendously.

In our everyday lives, as well as the lives of corporations, even major breakthroughs do not often result from single large steps or major changes. Rather, they result from many small improvements. Major innovations such as the transistor or airplane are rare. And even many of these major innovations may be traced back to many small discoveries which made them possible. Be willing to work toward major breakthroughs using small steps which minimize your risk.

Trying major new ideas for personal or business growth offers a major risk. Techniques such as Mind Energize and Mind Strengthen can help minimize this risk, as can prudent planning. However, when we change anything, some risk is involved. We as creative people must be willing to face some risk of failure if we are to grow personally or corporately. No change may involve more risk than change. For example, if another business is ruining us with competition, we'd better risk changing or we could lose everything.

Creativity Grows With Exercise!

1. Survey at least three people to determine what amount of their time is devoted to the pursuit of new ideas or trying new approaches.

2. Discuss the following quotation:

   "Spur not an unbroken horse, put not your ploughshare too deep into new land."   Sir Walter Scott

3. Use any three DO IT catalysts to help list at least ten reasons:

   a. why people need to pursue new ideas and try new approaches.

   b. why businesses are often unreceptive to the ideas of inventors.

   c. what inventors can do to reduce the resistance of companies to their new ideas.

4. List three ideas for each of the following:

   a. To what new areas could you apply your existing capabilities and assets?

   b. What new capabilities and assets do you see in others which might be fruitful for you to adopt?

   c. What new things can you develop in yourself which you don't observe in those around you?

d. In what ways might you present an idea to your boss to increase the chances that he will accept it?

Chapter 11

SUMMARY OF THE DO IT PROCESS AND CATALYSTS

The pattern of the DO IT process emphasizes the need to Define problems, Open yourself to many possible solutions, Identify the best solution and then Transform it into action effectively. The ten DO IT catalysts, designed to help us creatively define, open, identify and transform, are Mind Focus, Mind Grip, Mind Stretch, Mind Prompt, Mind Surprise, Mind Free, Mind Synthesize, Mind Integrate, Mind Strengthen and Mind Energize. The entire DO IT process and catalysts are summarized on the next two pages. Illustration 33 provides a visual picture of the DO IT process and catalysts.

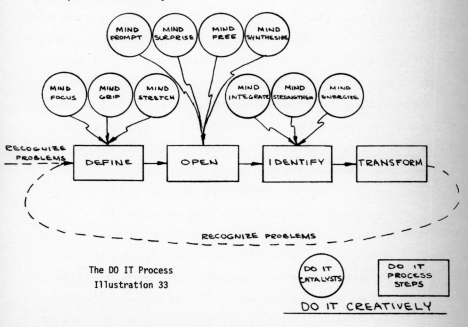

The DO IT Process
Illustration 33

-221-

As you found when reading this part of the text and doing the exercises, the DO IT catalysts can be of value individually as well as collectively. To use the entire DO IT process, all ten catalysts, and then to write down the answers, could require several hours. The results would be well worth it if the problem to be solved is a very important one or if the solution is one which you will spend a long time implementing. On the other hand, only a few minutes is required to benefit by using only some of the catalysts.

The investment of time in the use of DO IT process and catalysts is more than saved by obtaining the best idea, shortening the time to implement the idea, gaining confidence in our ideas, increasing the probability of success and reducing the extent of costly modifications which may have otherwise been necessary. It is worthwhile, from a personal growth point of view, to solve problems occasionally using the entire DO IT process and all the catalysts. As Somerset Maugham wrote, "Imagination grows with exercise." Use the DO IT catalysts, exercise your mind and increase the chance that you will automatically, habitually and routinely be creative in your everyday thinking. Place your mind on the pulse of your environment to recognize opportunities, aggravations and needs. Then do something about them. DO IT creatively.

The DO IT Process and Catalysts

(Define, Open, Identify and Transform Creatively)

NOTE: The DO IT catalysts may be used effectively separately for quick problem solving, or together as a process when very important or difficult problems are to be solved. They are designed to accelerate and strengthen your natural creative problem-solving ability and to stimulate a large number of good, diverse ideas for solutions to your problems.

Write down a statement of the problem!

Define the problem carefully to make sure you are solving the real problem and to help engage your unconscious and conscious minds to the problem.

Mind Focus
1) Ask why the problem exists. This may lead to a broader statement of the problem.
2) Try to subdivide the problem into smaller problems. This may lead to a narrower restatement of the problem.

Mind Grip
Write down at least three two-word statements of the problem objective. Select the combination of words which best represents the precise problem you want to solve. Use this to write a new, more optimal and effective restatement of the problem.

Mind Stretch
List the goals, objectives and/or criteria which the solution of the problem is to satisfy. (Think of obstacles which must be overcome.) Then stretch each goal, objective or criterion and write down any ideas which are stimulated.

Write down the most optimal statement of the problem.

Open yourself to consider many diverse solution ideas. Delay judgment on ideas generated until the Identify step. First, list any ideas which are on your mind. Then,

Mind Prompt
Ask other people with diverse backgrounds, knowledge and intelligence for solutions to your problem. Use their solutions as prompters for your own ideas.

Mind Surprise   List ridiculous, laughable ideas. Use them to
                   trigger more reasonable, possibly usable solutions
                   to your problem.

Mind Free   Stimulate fresh ideas by forcing similarities be-
                   tween your problem and things which aren't logically
                   related to your problem.
                   1) Write down the name of a physical object, pic-
                      ture, plant or animal.
                   2) List its characteristics in detail.
                   3) Use the listed characteristics to stimulate in-
                      sights into and ideas for the solution to your
                      problem.

Mind Synthesize   Use logical, haphazard and/or illogical combinations
                   of ideas already collected to stimulate new ideas.

Circle the best of ideas generated so far during the Define and Open steps.

   Identify the best solution to your problem and modify it until you are
ready to transform your idea into action.

Mind Integrate   Review your goals, objectives and/or criteria then
                   trust your own gut-level feeling to select the best
                   idea from the already circled ideas.

Mind Strengthen   List the negative aspects of your idea. Be vicious!
                   Try to positivize the negatives. Then modify the
                   solution to reduce the negative aspects.

Mind Energize   Exaggerate the worst and best potential consequence
                   which might result from the implementation of your
                   solution. Modify your solution to minimize bad con-
                   sequences and maximize good consequences. Proceed

-224-

to the transformation step if you are sufficiently
energized.

Carefully write down a statement of your final solution idea.

Transform your solution idea into action. Use the DO IT process
and catalysts again to help creatively solve the problem which you now
have of "How to transform your solution idea into action."

IMPORTANT NOTE: When time allows, take advantage of incubation (unconscious thinking) and research processes (find out what ideas have already
been tried).

Most of our everyday personal and professional problems are solved
in a few minutes or instantly. Therefore, you will probably find it advantageous to use only one or a few of the ten DO IT catalysts at a time.
You may want to clarify the problem's definition with Mind Focus, obtain
ideas from other people using Mind Prompt, or modify the final idea using Mind Strengthen. Perhaps you already have an idea and will use Mind
Energize to help you decide whether or not to transform it into action.
The entire DO IT process and any of the DO IT catalysts may be used to
help solve the problems, "In what ways can I transform this idea into
practice?"

The exercises which follow are provided to develop further skill
and insight into the DO IT catalysts and to provide the opportunity to
solve problems using various combinations of the catalysts.

Creativity Grows With Exercise!

1. Use Mind Focus, Mind Surprise and Mind Integrate to help solve the
    following problems:

    a. If you were an employer, what three questions would you ask of
        applicants to evaluate their creativity?

b. Design an automatic bird-food dispenser.

c. In what ways can I improve my public speaking ability?

2. Use Mind Strengthen and Energize to improve the following ideas:

a. A vacation on the beach.

b. A low cut tennis shoe.

c. Freeway or expressways.

3. Use the Mind Prompt and Mind Free to develop a list of at least ten possible solutions to the following problems:

a. In what ways can I decrease my tendency of self-criticism?

b. Design an adjustable baseball bat.

c. In what ways can I get more from this book?

4. Use Mind Grip, Surprise, Synthesize and Integrate to help solve the following problems. Develop at least twenty solution ideas for each problem before Mind integrating.

a. In what ways can children be encouraged to read more?

b. Design a device for picking up broken glass.

c. In what ways can I learn to relax better?

5. Use Mind Stretch, Mind Surprise and Mind Integrate to help solve the following problems:

a. What steps could a public library take to increase its use by the public?

b. In what ways can the design of a garage be improved?

c. Develop a motto for people who wish to think creatively.

6. Use all ten catalysts to help solve the following problems. Develop at least thirty solution ideas for each problem before entering the Identify phase of DO IT.

a. In what ways can a rubber band be used?

b. What factors might cause a successful business to fail?

c. In what ways can the design of a coffee table be improved?

d. What five useful things should drivers always have in their car?

e. In what ways can I contribute to the community in which I live?

f. What are my five best personal assets?

7. Develop a list of a hundred or more uses for:

a. A paper clip.

b. Velcro

c. A sponge.

8. Use any three creative catalysts to help develop forty solutions to the following problems:

a. In what ways can an inventor promote his product?

b. What reasons might an established automobile manufacturer offer for rejecting battery powered automobiles?

c. In what ways can you substantially reveal to other people that you are a practical creative thinker?

P A R T   I I I

RELATED TOPICS

In this part of the text, topics are presented which help to broaden and deepen your creativity. Quick creativity, which applies to predicaments and problems which need almost instant answers, is explored. The systematic use of groups for creative problem solving is presented. Ways to help you sustain your creativity after you have "closed" this book are discussed. Finally at the end of this section, the conclusion for the text is offered.

Chapter 12

QUICK CREATIVE THINKING
(Thinking Under Pressure)

The few minutes spent sitting in a dentist chair, waiting in the checkout line of a store, waiting for a bus, a waitress or a seat in a restaurant seems like a long time, and it is--especially when we compare it to the quickness of our mind.

Often times we give the excuse, "Things happen too fast, I can't think creatively." Not so! The central factors in creative thinking; thinking of good problems, defining problems well, developing alternative solutions and strengthening our ideas can all, or in part, be completed in a few minutes or seconds and can even be applied to helping us get out of predicaments which require "instant" answers.

The quick creativity of one of my college students occurred as follows, in his own words (dramatic words):

It was 6:30 a.m. The sun was rising above the end of the diving board. I felt aggressive enough to confidently dive off the diving board to newer heights. I started my "warm-up" by going through a previously planned list of dives, as I have done every day of every season for the past six years.

This was a particularly unique and important day because I was to compete in the Southern California College Diving Championships. I was almost finished with my first round through the "list." I was concentrating on doing an inward one and one-half somersault in a piked position. Upon completing the mental process of the diving, I was ready to start.

Standing on the end of the diving board backwards, I hung my heels horizontally off the board. Steadying my rhythm, I pressed the board and lifted high above it as I started propelling myself into the somersault. I remembered how the board was inappropriately positioned at a three-degree incline. This cursory thought was enough to warn me of the worst fate a diver can face - - - hitting the board with your head. My sudden reaction was to avoid the contact.

At this point, I was completing the first somersault and the ever-ending doom was coming into view. In an instant, I rationalized three options. Since my hands were holding the backs of my thighs, I could not fend off the collision of head-to-board. My options were; one, I could strike my face on the end of the board; two, choose my worst profile; three, tuck my head under with the chance of nicking the tip of the board with my head.

Unfortunately my downward momentum was faster than I anticipated. One of the coaches at the pool was a surgeon and he rushed me to the hospital to suture (stitch) my head in time to return for competition and a third-place trophy.

In a brief moment he was able to consciously consider three alternative solutions to his problem. Three alternatives are generally better and more creative than the usual one-solution idea.

You may have experienced alternate thinking in a brief amount of time. Often people who suddenly realize that they are unavoidably going to hit another car, or be hit by another car, have enough time to consider how to position themselves to minimize injury and/or how to minimize the damage to their car.

If you can't find a coffee stirrer, consider some alternative ways to stir coffee--a paper clip, toothpick, spoon or knife. These alternatives are generally considered better than the often used finger. If you find yourself faced with a large or small predicament, use your creativity to help you solve it. Creativity is an everyday sort of tool.

In my workshops and classes on creativity, participants are challenged with generally large numbers of alternatives to problems in one-, two- and three-minute time periods with generally good results. It is not unusual, if no time is taken to write down each answer, for a group of five people to develop fifty solution ideas.

The following problem solving results were achieved in three minutes for the problem, "In what ways can I be better to my friends and myself at the same time?" The mind thinks much faster than we can write. So, the fact that these solutions were thought of and written within a three-minute time span makes them more impressive. More often than not, you will find that you run out of ideas before you run out of time. Use Mind Free, Surprise and Synthesize to aid you when your idea well runs dry.

One student using Mind Focus restated the problem to read, "How can we improve ourselves and thereby become a better friend?" Possible solutions which he generated include: Improve personal hygiene, become more interesting, become aware of friends' interests, be a good listener, show an interest in a friend, wear a smile, take a trip, enroll in a course and be helpful. To be a good listener was selected as the best approach.

Another student left the problem stated as given. His ideas for solutions included: Be willing to help, respect other's privacy, be honest in social relationships, don't expect much from friends, don't give unsolicited advice, offer only constructive criticism and tell your friends dirty jokes. The chosen solution was to be honest in social relationships.

The intent of these examples is not to prove to you what great ideas these participants developed. Everyone has his or her own best solution to a problem of this nature. However, it is to show how much creative thinking can be compressed into a few minutes of time. Prove it to yourself. Try the exercises which follow:

Creativity Grows With Exercise!

1. In three minutes list as many solutions as you can for the following. Use Mind Surprise, Free and Synthesize to help you if you run out of ideas.

   a. List six introductory topics of conversation you might use to break the ice with a complete stranger.

   b. Your neighbors overhear you complaining about the color of their house. What things might you say to them if you want to remain friends?

   c. You are asked by a friend to contribute money to a charity which you don't like. What possible responses could you offer?

   d. The person standing next to you in line faints. What possible things could you do?

   e. You spill coffee on a sofa at a party. What things could you do to remedy the situation?

2. In two minutes mentally think of as many ideas as you can for the following problems. Write down the number of ideas you think of and the one or two you consider to be best.

   a. In what ways can teachers help students learn?

   b. You are sitting at home relaxing in your robe when your boss and his wife unexpectedly knock on the front door. What should you do?

   c. In what ways can families become closer and more harmonious?

   d. What pictures might be appropriate for the cover of a cookbook?

   e. You are suddenly brought into your boss's office. He regretfully explains that, due to a cutback in production, you must be fired. What possible things might you say at that time?

Chapter 13

GROUP CREATIVE PROBLEM SOLVING

In our society the role played by groups of all kinds such as con-
ferences, committees, teams, boards and clubs, is becoming increasingly
prevalent. Each of us is a part of, and frequently participates in,
group activity. Group thinking efforts are increasing rapidly, even
though they are frequently ineffective. This chapter is designed to
provide insights into group problem-solving efforts and ways to make them
effective.

Group Characteristics

Groups often function poorly because they place a premium on judgment and almost extinguish ideation, they don't separate judgment and
ideation and they harbor an illusion of effectiveness. Somehow, group
participants feel that because they agree on an idea, it must be the
best idea. They often feel they have reached an agreement when in fact
they have not. People as well as ideas are often attacked. They rarely
carefully define their objectives or problems to be solved and they often
adjourn their meeting before deciding on a plan of action.

The dominance of judgment over ideation during group meetings is
similar to that which occurs within each of us when we solve problems as
individuals. An idea is barely stated by a group member before it is
judged, then accepted or rejected. If it is accepted, it is often used
as the final solution. Any idea presented subsequently is handily rejected. If the initial idea is rejected, the process continues until
the group thinks they agree on some "better" idea. Ideas are considered
sequentially, one at a time. This is contrary to the creative way which

is to separate ideation from judgment, to generate many ideas while delaying judgment and then to select the best idea.

Once a group has selected an idea, they tend to exhibit an "illusion of quality." The idea is good because a large number of people thought of it. Therefore, the idea is protected and guarded from further criticism. The creative way is to use catalysts like Mind Strengthen and Energize to improve the idea. Attack the idea and modify it to make it stronger. Examine the consequences of implementing the idea and modify it to minimize the bad consequences and maximize the good ones.

The group selection process tends to be a bandwagon approach. Someone convincingly and with conviction presents the idea, another person nods his head in approval, no one offers another idea, the chairperson then proclaims, "That's it! This is the idea we will use." Little effort is made to systematically determine the strengths and weaknesses of the idea, to compare it directly with others or to genuinely determine if all of the group members really think that this is the best idea. Once an idea has momentum, few group members are willing to challenge it. Maybe the problem is solved, but is it the best solution?

Mind Prompting, with its selection grid, helps to overcome poor approaches to idea selection. Informal use of Robert's Rules of Order for offering an idea, asking for a second and calling for the question, though sometimes cumbersome and annoying, can correct the false sense of agreement problem associated with group selection processes.

The lack of proper problem definition discussed in Part II of this book applies equally to groups and individuals. Even if a group is effective at developing ideas, they often forget to carefully define the objectives of problems. When a problem is presented for solution, group members almost immediately begin to offer solution ideas. Virtually no effort is made to carefully define the problem or determine the constraints or criteria which affect it.

When a meeting ends, the participants often leave feeling like nothing constructive occurred even though great ideas were offered, spirited debates occurred and participants were intelligent, articulate and experienced. One reason is that no one usually takes the time to establish what should be done next, when or how to take the next step or who should do what. In other words, no plan was established.

Characteristics of Group Members. The outcome of group problem-solving efforts is directly dependent on the actions of the individual group members. Usually group members have experience, education and skills relevant to the topic of the meeting. However, they are generally poorly utilized. Participants don't listen to each other. They compete for the attention of the boss or leader. They are overly sensitive to criticism, quick to criticize others, and often more interested in supporting their own idea than finding the best idea.

Many people forcefully and enthusiastically defend your right to speak, but make little effort to listen. They may not listen because they are too busy collecting and preparing their own thoughts in preparation for their turn to speak. When they do listen, they often judge the idea and accept or reject it so quickly that they do not give it adequate consideration. Instead of playing with the idea or trying to build on it for a few minutes, they immediately react to it, usually negatively.

We are sensitive to criticism and often vindictive when it occurs. If someone discredits our idea, we often consciously or more often unconsciously lie in waiting for them to propose an idea so that we can "shoot it out of the saddle." This occurs frequently and is easily observed in a meeting. In fact, because we have been hurt by others' criticism during a meeting, we often consciously or unconsciously retaliate with a bigger weapon. We not only attack their ideas, we attack the people: "Only you could have made a suggestion like that," "My little sister suggested a similar approach," or, "That idea was used by the Romans just before the fall of Rome."

People want attention. Group members compete for the attention of the leader or the boss. Perhaps they want a promotion, more money for a pet project or simply recognition for their intelligence. Whatever the reason, group participants overtly or covertly, consciously or un--consciously, exhibit the competitive, "I win, you lose" approach. Getting the best idea is secondary to walking away a winner--feeling that your idea or criticisms were the best and that you are most admired by the leader and other participants.

Reasons for Group Meetings. The obstacles to productive group meetings presented by general group dynamics and participant characteristics are formidable. However, they aren't the only obstacles. Committee meetings and group problem-solving efforts are often conducted for other than the advertised purpose. A meeting, instead of being called to solve a problem, as appearances suggest, may actually be held to get support from a group of people for an already established idea, to falsely make people feel they are participating in the decision-making process, to satisfy the "company policy" that we have weekly meetings, or to share the blame with the group if anything goes wrong.

Often bosses and leaders call meetings to try to rally support behind their preconceived idea. They have planned a course of action but realize that "enlightened" contemporary management involves, even if superficially, employees or other forms of group membership in the decision making process. Usually employees can sense when they are involved in a meeting where the outcome is already predetermined and they respond accordingly (see illustration 34).

Creative Leadership?
Illustration 34

In addition to appearing like enlightened leaders, leaders get a "safety" benefit from meetings which are held to obtain group agreement for the preconceived idea. If the preconceived idea is successful, the leader takes full credit; if it fails, he reminds other people that it was not his idea after all - it was a "committee decision." They feel that they stand to lose nothing and gain everything. They often don't notice the low morale and half-hearted efforts of their employees during and after the meeting which are a result of their clumsy effort at genuine group thinking.

Many times, unfortunately, meetings are simply held, unenthusiatically and with no expectation of productivity, to comply with a company policy which requires "one meeting a week." The boss is annoyed by the input from his employees, the employees are bored with the unmeaningful deliberations, time is wasted, and morale lowered. Everyone is a loser.

Effective Group Meetings. Characteristics of poor meetings are not limited to meetings of secretaries, social clubs and clerks. They prevail in the highest level of business, government and education. In spite of all of the negative aspects of "normal" meetings, they are a very important and ever increasing part of our society. A good mental team, like a good physical team, when functioning properly, can do things which individuals cannot accomplish alone.

More minds think more thoughts. True, they often think the same or similar thoughts. However, psychological research, using devices such as word association tests and contrasting the efficiency of groups with individuals in problem solving, reveals that more minds also think up more singular, unique and original ideas. A study at the Buffalo campus of New York State University revealed that 70% more good ideas were developed by a group of brainstorming people than were generated by the same number of people working as individuals for the same period of time.

Effective group interaction involves sparks from one person's idea igniting an idea in another--much like Mind Prompting, a safe environment where all ideas are considered, a genuine concern for finding the best idea and transforming it into action, realization that problems need to be carefully defined, good listening habits, a creative leader and creative mixture of participants.

Group Composition and Size. Groups of people of similar age, education, experience, values, culture and professions tend to rigidify their pattern of thinking and narrow their range of ideas. For a creative group where many divergent, new ideas are to be developed before identifying the best one, an effort should be made to obtain group members with widely different capabilities and orientations.

If the problem is to invent a new type of pencil, include a mechanical engineer, industrial designer, marketing and production expert. However, pepper these salty experts with people with no experience in the area of the problem to be solved; a housewife, secretary, production foreman or expert from some other field during the ideation stage. This can provide a divergent element of ideation free from preconceived, traditional ideas. Utilize the experts to identify the best idea, modify it and plan for its transformation into action. Use the inexperienced people to sport unusual, wild, divergent lines of thinking.

Usually, five to seven people offers an optimum group size. Smaller groups tend to run out of ideas or may not include sufficient diversity. Larger groups tend to lead to individual apathy and inefficient use of personnel because there is not usually enough time in a meeting for individuals in larger groups to meaningfully contribute to the problem-solving effort.

Meeting Dynamics. The meeting should flow in an orderly fashion, providing for participation by all members, insuring good communications and separating ideation from judgment. It should be conducted in a problem solving fashion instead of in a discussion fashion. Rather than hold a meeting to discuss the need for higher employee morale, hold a meeting to solve the problem, "How can we best improve employee morale?" This problem-solving approach provides a more powerful focus of participants' efforts and leads to a more orderly, effective results-oriented meeting.

The DO IT process provides a pattern that can be used to bring order into a meeting. The group can first focus on defining the problem; then on obtaining many ideas while delaying judgment; next by identifying the best solution and strengthening it through modification; and finally, by focusing on a plan to transform it into action. The appropriate creative catalyst added to each of these phases can provide an effective, creative element to the group's efforts.

Participants should be encouraged to write down their ideas while they are waiting to express them. This helps clear their minds so that they may become better listeners to the ideas of others, to be clearer, more precise in the ultimate expression of their ideas and reduces the chance that they may forget their ideas before they have the opportunity to speak.

To promote a positive supportive atmosphere, participants should be encouraged to try to build on the ideas of others, use the constructive criticism of others, making the ideas stronger before trying to judge or criticize them. They should compete constructively by listing quantities of ideas and improvements of ideas during the ideation stage.

A secretary should be designated to insure that <u>all</u> good and bad ideas are recorded. When possible, the ideas should be recorded on a blackboard or flip chart paper visible to all of the group members to help reduce the repetition of ideas and stimulate new ideas. If the secretary is a full member of the group, it is often beneficial to rotate the secretarial role among the group members to provide empathy for the job of the secretary as a way to encourage all members to get involved and to prevent one person from being "stuck" with the task of being secretary.

Prior to the Open, ideation phases of group problem solving, a warm-up exercise can be helpful to help initiate more creative, free-wheeling type thinking and to underscore the principle of delaying judgment. As a warm-up, for five or ten minutes participants can be encouraged to use Mind Surprise or Free to generate ideas on problems such as: Name as many uses as you can for a coat hanger, brick, paper clip, toothpick or rubber band.

Mind Focus, Stretch and Grip should be used to help define the problem. However, with groups, especially highly homogeneous groups familiar with the types of problems you hope to solve, it can be useful to hide the identity of the actual problem statement until after the Open, ideation stage to reduce the chance that usual, habitual solutions to the problem will dominate the group. For example, if the problem is to design a new pencil sharpener and the group participants are all pencil sharpener designers, don't tell them what the real problem is. Instead begin by engaging them in a discussion on how to sharpen, point or grind things so that their preliminary ideas extend beyond the scope of traditional ways to sharpen pencils.

Group Leadership. The whole is equal to the sum of its parts. In mathematics this is true. In groups it is generally false. The group leader has by far the greatest opportunity and responsibility for insuring that the whole becomes more than the sum of its parts.

A good creative group leader effectively follows a plan such as the DO IT process to bring order into a meeting, gets most members of the group involved, protects individual egos while stimulating maximum productivity, listens carefully and does not dominate the meeting with his ideas, comments or observations.

The effective creative group leader does not inject his own ideas until after those of the group have been offered; he does not assume that he knows the real problem but enlists the aid of his group in the definition of the problem; he does not dismiss any idea offered as unworthy during the open phase; he restrains himself from showing partiality for any particular idea generated; he uses smiles, nods and verbal prompters to reward and stimulate ideas; he tries to clarify and simplify ideas, and is forceful but gentle in his leadership.

How does one become a good leader? By practice and through experience! Probably the most difficult skill of a leader is to gently, without offending individual members, keep the group focused on the problem and phase of the problem solving currently being considered. When the leader is trying to develop a well defined problem statement, many members will offer solutions. While the leader is trying to collect ideas and encourage members to delay judgment, many members will be critical, will select ideas or try to contemplate a plan of action.

Robert's Rules of Order can provide a very stultifying, dulling uncreative flare to a meeting. However, at the point of idea identification, it is extremely important to use the move, second and call for the question approach to insure that the best idea is selected and that most group members agree. Otherwise the groups often work under an "illusion of unanimity" where the chairman feels that everyone likes one particular idea. This feeling is often incorrect and is based on the enthusiasm and authority of only a few group members. If the problem is one which must be implemented by the leader, or where one member has a much greater expertise than the others, he should choose the final best solution.

<u>Creativity Grows With Exercise!</u> (Group Exercises)

Use any of the following formats to work on exercises 2 through 6:

    a. Group consisting of two people.

    b. Group consisting of five to seven people.

    c. Group consisting of ten or more people.

1. What are five good methods a group leader could use to encourage a quiet member of the group to participate?

2. What are five good methods a group leader could employ to keep an unusually vocal group member from dominating the session?

3. Invent a better book storage unit for a businessman's office.

4. In what ways can people improve their ability to listen well?

5. What improvements can be made to the family room in a home?

6. In what ways can we get people involved in their local parent-teacher organization?

7. Conduct a "stop and go" group problem solving session on problems 1 through 6. For five minutes collect as many ideas as possible, have a silent pause for incubation, five minutes more for ideas, then five minutes to identify the best solution and, finally, modify it to strengthen it.

8. Use all nine of the DO IT catalysts as a group on a problem of the group's choice.

9. As a group, list at least twenty-five solutions to a problem of your choice. Each member should then privately write down the idea he identifies as the best. Compare the selections of the group. Is there unanimity? Discuss the possible reasons for similarities and differences in the choices.

10. State a problem. Have all members of the group privately rewrite the

problem in what they consider to be a clear statement form. Compare the restatements. Are they the same problem? Would they have a similar solution?

11. Solve the problem, "In what ways can I be positive?" Have each member of the group offer a solution. Ask the person to the right of the ideating one to restate the essence of the idea offered. Do people listen well? Are they able to capture the essence of someone else's idea?

12. Invite an outside expert such as a businessman, inventor or poet to your problem solving session. Ask him to bring a problem for you to help him solve. Use Mind Focus and Surprise to help with the solution. Let him select the best answer. Then use Mind Strengthen to help modify the selected idea.

13. Observe a group leader in action. List three positive and three negative aspects of his leadership.

14. Observe a group in action. Try to answer the following questions:

a. Did they define the problem?

b. Did they listen to each other?

c. Did they separate judgment and ideation?

d. Did they compete with each other?

e. Did all group members get involved?

f. Did one member dominate the group?

g. Did they follow some organized procedure?

h. In what ways could the leader have improved the effectiveness of the group?

Chapter 14

SUSTAINING YOUR CREATIVITY

Erosion doesn't only happen to mountains - it happens to creativity when it is not used. If we don't properly feed and exercise our creativity, it becomes flabby, unresponsive and lazy. Becoming more creative is a life-long process.

Changes in our environment, contacts, reading, activities, hobbies and sports can help feed our creativity. Exercise and plain old practice can maintain the strength and responsiveness of our creativity. Proper planning can help insure that we do exercise. Helping other people be more creative also helps our own creativity.

Taking vacations at different locations, eating at different restaurants, meeting new people with varying backgrounds, reading books, magazines and newspaper articles on topics we don't usually read about, trying different hobbies and sports often provide the freshness, vitality and sparks which help feed our everyday and professional creativity.

Sheer practice will increase our creativity (see illustration 35). If we practice kindness we tend to be kinder, good cheer helps us become more cheerful and practicing creativity helps us become more creative. Your creativity can be exercised by thinking up solutions to specific problems. They don't have to be real problems, although those are the most motivating and rewarding.

Just as jogging ten to fifteen minutes a day can exercise your body and dramatically improve your physical health, exercising your mind by creatively solving problems for ten to fifteen minutes a day can dramatically improve your natural creativity.

Set aside a definite period of time each day or night for creative thinking. It can be done before breakfast, lunch or dinner, while commuting, or during a coffee break. Try different times to see what works best for you.

Creativity Flourishes and Grows With Exercise
Illustration 35

One study of joggers revealed that twice as many people who began jogging at night gave up as those who jogged in the morning. The morning does tend to be the best time to think for most people. But remember, we are all individuals. Many people don't mentally awaken until noontime.

Try to find an environment which is conducive to creative exercise. For some it may be a separate quiet room, others the center of a congested cafeteria and others a car or bus. Try several environments to determine what works best.

Creativity does grow with exercise. There is no doubt about it! However, the cruel truth is that to spend time each day for exercise requires almost superhuman capabilities. I jog usually three or four times each week. I enjoy jogging and the mental, physical and emotional benefits which it provides me. Yet, I will go off the target and not jog for months. Very few people I know are consistent in jogging, meditation, praying or any other beneficial but artificially forced daily routine.

That doesn't mean that we give up. Creative exercise for one day a week is better than none or a few days a year. If you fail at consistent creative exercise, try again. That's the creative way. If it is important enough to you, you will do it.

Often we aren't creative because we forget to be creative and we forget the many benefits that it produces for ourselves and others. One of the benefits of going to church is that it reminds us to be good and about the value of being good. Meditation advocates often meditate immediately before breakfast. Religious people often pray just prior to going to sleep. The success of this daily routine is given an initial start by the triggering or reminding effect of an event--breakfast or going to sleep--and then eventually sustained by habit.

Other triggering reminders for religious people may be a Bible on the mantel or, for the meditator, a picture of the Maharishi Yogi in their wallet. These reminders are similar to tying a string around your finger to remind you to buy milk at the store. Clever sayings, symbols, artwork and sculpture can be used as reminders. They can be placed on the bathroom mirror, in the kitchen, car or office.

Helping others become more creative is also a way to help sustain your own creativity. I am lucky. My creative problem-solving writing, lectures, courses and workshops which help others are very beneficial to me. One person's creative thinking releases others'.

One way to help others be more creative is to accept their first idea as possibly a good idea, but then ask for more ideas and other possibilities. Demonstrate to them the value of quantity to get quality and delaying judgment. Listen carefully to what they say and encourage them to do the things that they have always talked about. Invite them to try new and different sports, vacations and readings.

The only drawback in trying to help others is that we often use that as an excuse to not help ourselves. As the ancient Hebrew saying suggests; what I am telling others, I am not telling myself. As with the coach below, he is exercising the body of his athletes but neglecting his own.

Do As I Say!
Illustration 36

Creativity Grows With Exercise!

1. Discuss the following statements.

    a. Do the world's most successfully creative people have difficulty in maintaining their creativity after they become famous and prosperous? Why?

    b. Creativity often erodes away.

    c. Physical and mental exercising can be conducted in a similar fashion.

2. Daily, for one week, schedule and apply the DO IT process and catalysts to problems of your choice. Spend five minutes each day or enough time to develop fifteen solution ideas for the problem under consideration.

3. In what ways can we exercise our creativity while doing the following regular activities of our lives:

    a. Reading.

    b. Riding in a car pool.

    c. Watching T.V.

    D. Reading the newspaper.

    e. At work.

    f. Doing yard work.

    g. Doing housework.

    h. Jogging.

    c. Playing a sport.

4. In what ways can we, without being offensive or obvious, help improve and exercise the creativity of:

    a. Our family.

    b. Friends.

c. Spouse.

d. Boss.

e. Employees.

5. What objects, plaques or other items could we place around our home or office to help remind us to be more creative?

6. What environment best stimulates your creativity? List twenty possibilities and select the most likely two or three specific environments. Why?

7. During what period of the day are you most creative? Second most? Third most?

8. Are you more creative on the job, weekends, at parties, with your family or while playing a sport or working at a hobby? Why?

9. How do the following people improve and exercise their creativity?

a. Artists.

b. Composers.

c. Engineers.

d. Architects.

e. Businessmen.

f. Teachers.

g. Writers.

10. Try to be completely habitual and totally uncreative for a day. Discuss the results.

11. What games could be developed to exercise creativity?

Chapter 15

SUMMARY AND CONCLUSION

There is creativity within individual people--not society, schools, political systems or business--but in you and me. Everyone is creative. All it takes to become more creative is a little push, a little assurance, some exercise, an eye for problems and alternatives to their solution. We can develop these abilities.

We are like a large object in motion - we resist change. Habits, like comfortable shoes, fit our daily grind and establish our unconscious and conscious prejudgments. To be creative is to be ready to consider new possibilities, different ideas and alternative approaches. It requires that, when we feel something new is right, we do something with it. We don't have to wear the worn-out shoe of habit into incompetence, blandness and indecisiveness.

Change is basic to our society. It often results from new demands and needs for more energy, a more fruitful life, a need of peace or new friendships. Instead of just trying to react to and to "keep up" with change, we as creative people need to control change and direct it so that it is most beneficial to man on earth.

Creativity is not out of touch with reality, only for the frivolous, to be used only in times of emergency. It is a tool to reach out and say, "I am somebody," "I feel a need to and will contribute to society," "Life can be better." It is a way of overcoming and outsmarting concrete problems in business, governments, the arts and personal living.

Ethel Barrymore once said, "It's what you learn after you know it all that counts." Expanding and using your creativity helps you to do something--transform into action that which you already know. It's not what you know that counts; it's what you do with what you know.

You don't have to be creative every moment of your life. Habit is necessary to physical, mental and emotional survival. Like large corporations which invest one percent of their budget in research, be creative one percent of the time. It only takes a few minutes a day. Be creative in your leisure, work and social activities. Don't save it for just weekends or only on the job. These apparently small deliberate investments of creativity can yield profitable solutions to problems and lead to a natural, habitual creative approach which permeates your existence.

The value of doing something, anything, has been stressed in this book. You can think about things forever and have great ideas, but accomplish nothing. Becoming more creative does involve the risk of failure, uncertainty and just plain hard work. Every new thing is met with resistance. You do have to perspire to complete things. But it's better than rusting away in habits.

If you drive home after reading this book today, don't think too much about the DO IT process or Mind Surprising--you may crash. We spend most of our time focusing on the reality of everyday life. One of the often missed realities is that we need to be creative some of the time if we are to be happy, healthy, productive people. To keep ourselves on an even keel and sane, we do need to walk that delicate line between too much habit and too much creativity, too great a risk and too little a risk, taking ourselves too seriously and being too frivolous. A sensitive awareness of our environment, our inner and outer selves and experience help us walk this line.

By reading this book now and limbering and strengthening your mind with its exercises, you have rediscovered, sped up and made new creative approaches to facing and conquering problems. It has helped provide that little push everyone needs. It has helped your life become more fun, exciting and rewarding.

I hope you have experienced the value of flexible, fluid thinking, tapping your unconscious resource, recognized the value of "gut-level" feelings, quantity to get diversity and quality, careful problem definition and strengthening of the solution. The catalysts and processes for deliberate creativity which you have experienced in this book are not fixed and inflexible. They can and should be changed, modified, tailored and customized to meet your specific needs and capitalize on your unique resources and capabilities.

Don't ignore any possible catalyst or stimulus to creativity. Occasionally review old ones and try new ones. The fundamentals of deliberate creativity presented in this book are based on the experience and styles of great creative thinkers. Stand on the shoulders of giants. Learn from them. But in the end, select and use what fits your particular needs.

Many of us spend our lives in futile rebellion against things we cannot change, in passive habitual acceptance of things that we can change and never try to learn the difference. The prayer attributed to the theologian Reinhold Niebuhr, "God grant me the serenity to accept the things I cannot change, courage to change the things I can, and wisdom to know the difference," provides a good summary of one of the goals of a creative person. It's not easy to achieve. Experience will

help. But you have to <u>do</u> <u>something</u> to gain experience - even if it's
wrong.

"Every goal man reaches provides a new starting point, and the sum
of all man's days is just a beginning," observed Lewis Mumford. Your
opportunities to be creative are here and now. Set your goals, plan time
for creative practice, solve problems creatively and make your life more
interesting, productive and adventuresome. Don't stop. As Goethe said,
"He only earns his freedom and existence who daily conquers them anew."

Don't wait for others. Go ahead. Now it's up to you. Don't stop
now. As Bishop Richard Cumberland observed, "It is better to wear out
than to rust out." Be creative--don't let your habit kill you. You have
plenty of room for growth. Man often dies before he is fully born.

The role of self-concept in personal behavior is well established
in psychology. If we think we are failures, we tend to fail. If we
think we are good, we tend to be good. And if we think we are creative,
we tend to be creative. Everyone is creative. The more you feel that
you are creative, the more you will be creative.

Sounds easy doesn't it? If we have a creative attitude, think we
are creative and persist in our actions, we will be a creative success.
All fat people know that to reduce, they simply must reduce their level
of food intake. Heavy smokers and alcoholic drinkers can add years to
their life by simply stopping their self-destructive behavior. It is
not easy. However, it is not an "all or nothing" situation in creativity.
If we just recognize that we can be creative and apply it to small situations, we will be creative. We can uncrate our own creativity (see
illustration 37).

Uncrate the Create!
Illustration 37

Appendix

General Problems for Creative Growth

Educational

1. In what ways can we reduce the cost of used books in college book stores?
2. In what ways can we keep educators up-to-date with respect to the current practices of business and industry?
3. In what ways can students be motivated to learn more in school?
4. In what ways can the community be involved in the public education process?
5. What types of new courses should be introduced into college, high school and/or elementary school education?
6. In what ways can we continue our education after we graduate?
7. In what ways can we reduce the cost of college education?
8. In what ways can students improve their study habits?
9. In what ways can we finance public education?
10. In what ways can we determine whether a student is fit to graduate from elementary school, high school or college?

Societal

1. In what ways can we encourage the young to respect and be more concerned with the well-being of the elderly?
2. In what ways can we encourage people to be nicer to each other?
3. In what ways can urban centers be revitalized?
4. In what ways can we insure a proper balance of governmental regulations and free enterprise?
5. In what ways can we help the poor without making them helpless?
6. In what ways can we contribute to world peace?
7. In what ways can we strengthen the inner cities?
8. In what ways can we utilize the greatest strengths of each individual to develop a better nation?
9. In what ways can we insure the welfare of people after they retire?
10. What can be done in society to help insure that all men are treated fairly and equally?

Everyday Living

1. In what ways can we vent our anger safely?
2. In what ways can we eat better?
3. In what ways can we find a good balance between work and play?
4. In what ways can we keep ourselves healthier?
5. In what ways can we contribute to the well-being of friends, employers, employees or society in general?
6. In what ways can family life be made more exciting and stimulating?
7. In what ways can we make our life more exciting?
8. In what ways can we be happier?
9. What goals should we have in life?
10. In what ways can we help ourselves tune in to the "here and now"?

Business and Management

1. Think of ten new possible service businesses.
2. Think of twenty ways to sell ice cream.
3. In what ways can absenteeism of production workers be reduced?
4. In what ways can we strengthen the free enterprise system?
5. In what ways can businesses better communicate to the public their positive contribution to society?
6. In what ways can supervisors communicate better with their employees?
7. In what ways can department stores reduce shoplifting?
8. In what ways can the toil be removed from managers', production workers' or professionals' working hours?
9. In what ways can businesses help employees keep current with developments which are relevant to and might improve their work?
10. In what ways can management fairly and effectively evaluate its employees?

Medical and Physical

1. In what ways can doctors reduce the number of malpractice suits?
2. In what ways can people choose a doctor or dentist?
3. What preventative steps can we take to help prevent illness?
4. In what ways can the cost of medical care be reduced?
5. In what ways can the volume of forms for medical insurance be reduced?
6. In what ways can the waiting time at doctors' and dentists' offices be reduced?
7. What can be done in schools to improve the physical condition of students?

8. How do you choose a diet?
9. In what ways can nurses and paramedics be used to better augment the work of the doctor?
10. In what ways can patients be better prepared for a visit to the doctor?

Law Enforcement and Legal

1. In what ways can burglarizing in suburbs be reduced?
2. In what ways can individuals become more aware of their legal rights?
3. In what ways can policemen and/or lawyers improve their public image?
4. In what ways can courts reduce their legal load?
5. How do you select a competent lawyer for an automobile injury case?
6. What unnecessary functions do policemen currently perform?
7. In what ways can policemen enforce freeway speed limits?
8. What can be done to reduce shoplifting in department stores?
9. In what ways can legal fees be reduced?
10. What steps can be taken to keep drunk drivers off the freeway?

Creativity

1. Invent a new group or individual deliberate catalyst for stimulating creativity.
2. What item in nature is most symbolic of creativity?
3. In what ways can the creativity of elementary school children be increased?
4. In what ways should a creative person spend his vacation?
5. Invent a toy to stimulate creative thinking in adults.
6. What legislation could be enacted by congress to improve people's creative thinking?
7. What are some characteristics of a creative marriage?
8. In what ways can senior citizens be creative?
9. In what ways can policemen be more creative?
10. In what ways can we be creative at meal times?

Invention

1. What improvements could be made to a car to make it more comfortable?
2. What improvements could be made to a car to make it more reliable?
3. What improvements could be made to a car to make it more economical?
4. Design a container for bobby pins.
5. Design a container for safety pins.

6. Design a container for toothpicks.
7. Design an automatic dog feeding machine.
8. Invent a better pan for frying eggs.
9. Invent a new and entertaining pencil holder.
10. Invent a new adult board game.
11. Invent a new educational toy for preschool, elementary and/or high school students.
12. Design a jumping toy.

Political

1. What imaginary headlines would you like to see in the paper tomorrow? Select one headline. What could be done to make that headline a reality?
2. In what ways can we make governmental representatives more representative of individuals they represent?
3. In what ways can outstanding people be encouraged to enter politics?
4. In what ways can we improve the current approach to political campaigning to provide the voter with a clearer picture of the candidate?
5. In what ways can we reduce voter apathy for national elections?
6. In what ways can U.S. Senators maintain close contact with the constituency?
7. In what ways can campaign funds be obtained?
8. In what ways can we as individuals change the way the congress functions?
9. In what ways can cities maintain their autonomy from the state and federal government?
10. What can be done to prevent corruption in government?

Future

1. What type of transportation system should we have in major cities in the next thirty years?
2. In what ways will family life change in the next thirty years?
3. What three things would you want to change in the world within the next twenty years?
4. What changes will occur in education in the next twenty years?
5. In what ways will people be more creative twenty years from now?

Engineering

1. Of what value to man is the space program?
2. In what ways can the negative impact of freeways and expressways on their immediate environment be minimized?
3. In what ways can automobiles be made safer?
4. In what ways can technology help the medical profession?
5. In what ways can engineers keep ahead of current developments?
6. In what ways can dams be built with minimum negative impact on the environment?
7. In what ways can we provide electricity to a remote desert location?
8. In what ways can we use the potential energy of a river?
9. In what ways can we provide water to a desert region?
10. In what ways can people be encouraged to conserve energy?

Architectural

1. What would a wealthy person's bathroom contain that middle class bathrooms don't?
2. In what ways can the square foot costs of single family residences be reduced?
3. In what ways can architects become more efficient?
4. In what ways can governmental bodies expedite construction plan approvals?
5. In what ways can land costs be made more reasonable?
6. What architectural designs help save energy?
7. In what ways can computers help the architectural profession?
8. In what ways can architects be stimulated to keep aware of current developments?
9. In what ways can architectural draftsmen be better utilized?
10. In what ways can architects encourage commercial and large-scale residential developers to make better use of their services?

Career

1. What new careers have emerged in the last decade?
2. What would you do with your life if you could retire from your present job next week?
3. What career would you choose if you were not concerned about how much money you might earn?

4. What career would you choose if you only cared about making money?
5. What careers offer the greatest variety of experience?
6. What careers offer the least variety of experience?
7. What careers offer the greatest possibility of creative expression?
8. What careers offer the least possibility of creative expression?
9. What careers offer no possibility of creative expression?
10. What careers provide the greatest verbal interaction with other people?

Ecological

1. In what ways can individuals conserve energy?
2. In what ways can people reduce the amount of garbage they generate?
3. In what ways can air pollution in urban centers be reduced?
4. In what ways can growing cities control and guide their growth?
5. In what ways can the littering of national parks by campers be reduced?
6. In what ways can highway noise be reduced?
7. In what ways can we finance the preservation of historical landmarks in a small community?
8. In what ways can we encourage people to take personal responsibility for their impact on the environment?
9. In what ways can we save the prime agricultural land from being covered with homes and industries?
10. In what ways can we reduce the average amount of miles driven by people in automobiles in this country?

Bibliography

Arnspiger, V. Clyde, W. Ray Rucker and Mary E. Preas, _Personality in Social Process: Values and Strategies of Individuals in a Free Society_. Dubuque, Iowa, W. C. Brown Book Company, 1961.

Barron, Frank, _Creativity and Personal Freedom_. Princeton, New Jersey, D. Van Nostrand, Inc., 1968

Flesch, Rudolf, Ph.D., _The Art of Clear Thinking_. New York, Barnes and Noble Books, 1951.

Gallwey, W. Timothy, _The Inner Game of Tennis_. New York, Random House, 1974.

Ghiselin, Brewster, _The Creative Process: A Symposium_. Berkeley, California, 1952.

Gordon, W. J. J., _Synectics_. New York, Harper & Row, 1961.

Kubie, Lawrence S., M.D., _Neurotic Distortion of the Creative Process_. New York, The Noonday Press, 1961.

Lowen, Alexander, M.D., _Pleasure: A Creative Approach to Life_. New York, Penguin Books, 1970.

McKim, Robert H., _Experiences in Visual Thinking_. Monterey, Calif., Brooks/Cole Publishing Co., 1972.

Maslow, A. H., _Motivation and Personality_. New York, Harper & Row, Publishers, 1954.

May, Rollo, _The Courage to Create_. New York, W. W. Norton and Company, 1975

Moustakas, Clark, The Merrill-Palmer Institute, _Creativity and Conformity_. New York, D. Van Nostrand Company, 1967.

Osborn, Alex R., L.H.D., _Applied Imagination_. New York, Scribner's Sons, 1963.

Osborn, Alex R., L.H.D., _How to Become Creative: 101 Rewarding Ways to Develop Your Potential Talent_. New York, Scribner's Sons, 1964.

Parnes, Sidney, _Creative Behavior Guidebook_. New York, Scribner's Sons, 1967.

Prince, George M., _The Practice of Creativity A Manual for Dynamic Group Problem Solving_. New York, Harper & Row Publishers, 1970.

Von Fonge, Eugene E., _Professional Creativity_. Englewood Cliffs, N.J., Prentice-Hall, 1959.